Technician's Formulation Handbook for Industrial and Household Cleaning Products

Henry J Hannan

Kyral LLC, Waukesha, Wisconsin

Kyral LLC
Waukesha, Wisconsin

Printed 2007

All rights reserved. No part of this book may be reproduced, stored in a retrieval system, or transcribed, in any form or by any means-electronic, mechanical, photocopying, recording, or otherwise-without the prior written permission of the publisher, Kyral LLC.

Copyright 2007

ISBN 978-0-6151-5601-9

The information given in this book is for educational and informational purposes only. This book is meant to give a quick start to research by other professionals, but it should absolutely not be relied upon for any purposes whatsoever. We make NO GUARANTEES as to the accuracy of the information herein and you should not rely on it. Even professionals who use this information must independently verify whether it is correct and current.

Preface

Present textbooks of formulation chemistries fall into two broad categories. The first are manufacture's formulations that focus on selling their products to blenders or manufactures of cleaning products. The second are advanced formulation texts that focus on experienced formulators. This handbook is intended for beginning formulators and chemical technicians; it covers basic physical characteristics used in formulations, base chemicals that are typically used in cleaning products, such as: acid, bases, solvents, and surfactants. This handbook also covers the basics in analysis and experimental methods useful in product development and quality control. This handbook also includes formulations which have been established to provide functional performance criteria in the appropriate industry. The base formulations include cleaning products for industrial, household, and automotive applications. Each formulation lists information on raw material percentage by weight or volume, key properties, and more.

The target audiences for this handbook are chemical technicians and managerial personnel involved in training of personnel in development cleaning products. This would also include the end costomers, manufacturing companies and firms who supply raw materials or services to these companies.

Contents

Physical Properties	6
Substances and Mixtures	21
Acid (Mineral)	22
Organic Acids	33
Base/Alkali	38
Borax	43
Chlorides	44
Fluorides	48
Nitrates	49
Phosphates	50
Silicates	51
Sulfates	52
Solvents	54
Amines	62
Surfactants	64
Emulsions	72
Surfactants Types and Applications	74
Amphoteric	75
Anionic	78
Cationic	82
Nonionic	84
Phosphate Esters	89

Specialty Surfactants	90
Silicone Fluids	91
Chelation	91
Experiment/Testing Method	93
Analysis Methods	97
Chemical Mixing	114
Industrial and Household Formulations	119
Industrial Cleaners	119
Metal Cleaners and Lubricants	133
Household Cleaning Products	141
Rug, Carpet and Floor Care	152
Automotive Care Products	162
Appendix	171
References	202
INDEX	204

PHYSICAL PROPERTIES

The physical properties of the components in formulations are especially important. Knowledge of the characteristics of the components allows the formulator to choose the proper ingredients to create the desired product. Basic physical properties in formulating products are density, viscosity, solubility, polarity, miscibility, pH, color, odor, flash point, boiling point, freezing point, and surface tension.

DENSITY

For a homogeneous object, the formula **Mass/Volume** may be used. The mass is normally measured with an appropriate scale; the volume may be measured directly (from the geometry of the object) or by the displacement of a liquid. A very common instrument for the direct measurement of the density of a liquid is the hydrometer. The density is determined by the mass m per unit volume **V**. For the common case of a homogeneous substance, it is expressed as:

$$P = \frac{M}{V}$$

where, in SI units:
P is the density of the substance, measured in kg·m-3
M is the mass of the substance, measured in kg
V is the volume of the substance, measured in m3

Typically in a laboratory setting the best practice measuring the test solution is by hydrometer at a specified temperature. A quick measuring technique to determine the specific gravity of the test solution is by volumetric flask. This technique is based on mass volume, first tare the weight of the flask, and then fill the flask to volume and then weight the flask. Divide the weight by the volume of the volumetric flask. This method is not exact because it is difficult to prevent excess material from adhering onto the sides of the flask during transfer of the test solution. [1, 6, 21]

VISCOSITY

Viscosity is a measure of the resistance of a fluid to distort under shear stress. It is perceived as "thickness", or resistance to flow. Viscosity describes a fluid's internal resistance to flow and may be thought of as a measure of fluid friction. As an example, water is a lower viscosity liquid while vegetable oil is a higher viscosity liquid. All fluids have resistance to shear stress; an ideal fluid has no resistance to shear stress. When looking at a value for viscosity the number that one most often sees is the coefficients of viscosity (the ratio between the pressure exerted on the surface of a fluid, in the lateral or horizontal direction, to the change in velocity of the fluid as you move down in the fluid-referred as a velocity gradient).

Newton postulated that, for straight, parallel and uniform flow, the shear stress, τ, between layers is proportional to the velocity gradient, $\partial u/\partial y$, in the direction perpendicular to the layers, in other words, the relative motion of the layers.

$$T = \eta \frac{\partial u}{\partial y}$$

Here, the constant η is known as the coefficient of viscosity, the viscosity, or the dynamic viscosity. Many fluids, such as water and most gases satisfy Newton's criterion and are known as Newtonian fluids. Non-Newtonian fluids exhibit a more complicated relationship between shear stress and velocity gradient than simple linearity.

Viscosity is measured with various types of viscometer. Close temperature control of the fluid is essential to accurate measurements, particularly in materials like lubricants, whose viscosity (-40 < sample temperature <0) for example can change double in only 5 deg. C. For some fluids, it is a constant over a wide range of shear rates. The fluids without a constant viscosity are called Non-Newtonian fluids.

In paint industries, viscosity is commonly measured with a Zahn cup, in which the efflux time is determined and given to customers. The efflux time can also be converted to kinematic viscosities (cSt) through the conversion equations. Also used in paint, a Stormer viscometer uses load-based rotation in order to determine viscosity. It uses units, Krebs units (KU), unique to this viscometer.

The SI physical unit of dynamic viscosity is the pascal-second (Pa·s), which is identical to 1 kg·m−1·s−1. For example if a fluid with a viscosity of one Pa·s is placed between two plates, and one plate is pushed sideways with a shear stress of one pascal, it moves a distance equal to the thickness of the layer between the plates in one second.

The cgs physical unit for dynamic viscosity is the poise named after Jean Louis Marie Poiseuille. It is more commonly expressed, particularly in ASTM standards, as centipoise (cP). The centipoise is commonly used because water has a viscosity of 1.0020 cP (at 20 °C; the closeness to one is a convenient coincidence). The relation between Poise and Pascal-second is:

10 P = 1 kg·m−1·s−1 = 1 Pa·s

$$1 \text{ cP} = 0.001 \text{ Pa·s} = 1 \text{ mPa·s}$$

Kinematic viscosity (Greek symbol: ν) has SI units ($m^2 s^{-1}$). The cgs physical unit for kinematic viscosity is the stokes (abbreviated S or St), named after George Gabriel Stokes. It is sometimes expressed in terms of centistokes (cS or cSt). In U.S. usage, stoke is sometimes used as the singular form. [3, 4, 5]

$$1 \text{ stokes} = 100 \text{ centistokes} = 1 \text{ cm}^2 \cdot s^{-1} = 0.0001 \text{ m}^2 \cdot s^{-1}.$$
$$1 \text{ centistokes} = 1 \text{ mm}^2/s$$

pH

pH is a measure of the acidity or alkalinity of a solution. Solutions with a pH less than seven are considered acidic, while those with a pH greater than seven are considered basic (alkaline). The pH of 7 is considered neutral because it is the accepted pH of pure water at 25 °C (pure water cannot be assigned a pH value). pH is formally dependent upon the activity of hydrogen ions (H^+), but for very pure dilute solutions, the molarity may be used as a substitute with some sacrifice of accuracy. Because pH is dependent on activity, a property which cannot be measured easily or predicted theoretically, it is difficult to determine an accurate value for the pH of a solution. The pH reading of a solution is usually obtained by comparing unknown solutions to those of known pH, and there are several ways of doing this.

pH is shorthand for its mathematical approximation: in chemistry a small p is used in place of writing $-\log_{10}$ and the H should more correctly be $[H^+]$, standing for concentration of hydrogen ions. In simpler terms, the number arises from a measure of the activity of hydrogen ions in the solution. The pH scale is a reverse logarithmic representation of relative hydrogen proton (H^+) concentration. Unlike linear scales that progress in a smooth, incremental manner, a shift in value on the pH scale represents a tenfold difference in H^+ concentration. For example, a shift in pH from 2 to 3 represents a 10-fold decrease in H^+ concentration, and a shift from 2 to 4 represents a one-hundred (10×10)-fold decrease in H^+ concentration. The formula for calculating pH is:

$$pH = -\log_{10} a_{H^+}$$

Where a_{H^+} denotes the activity of H^+ ions, and is dimensionless. In solutions that contain other ions, activity and concentration are not the same. The activity is an effective concentration of hydrogen ions, rather than the true concentration; it accounts for the fact that other ions surrounding the hydrogen ions will shield

Substance	pH
Hydrochloric Acid, 10M	-1.0
Lemon juice	2.4
Cola	2.5
Vinegar	2.9
Orange juice	3.5
Beer	4.5
Coffee	5.0
Tea	5.5
Milk	6.5
Pure Water	7.0
Seawater	7.7 – 8.3
Hand soap	9.0 – 10.0
Household ammonia	11.5
Bleach	12.5
Household lye	13.5

them and affect their ability to participate in chemical reactions. These other ions effectively change the hydrogen ion concentration in any process that involves H+ ion.

In dilute solutions (such as tap water), the activity is approximately equal to the numeric value of the concentration of the H+ ion, denoted as [H+] (or more accurately written, [H3O+]), measured in moles per liter (also known as molarity). Therefore, it is often convenient to define pH as:

$$pH \approx -\log_{10} \frac{[H+]}{1\ mol/L}$$

For both definitions, log10 denotes the base-10 logarithm; therefore pH defines a logarithmic scale of acidity. In solution at 25 °C, a pH of 7 indicates neutrality (i.e. the pH of pure water) because water naturally dissociates into H+ and OH− ions with equal concentrations of 1×10−7 mol/L. A lower pH value (for example pH 3) indicates increasing strength of acidity, and a higher pH value (for example pH 11) indicates increasing strength of basicity. Note, however, that pure water, when exposed to the atmosphere, will take in carbon dioxide, some of which reacts with water to form carbonic acid and H+, thereby lowering the pH to about 5.7.

Neutral pH at 25 °C is not exactly 7. pH is an experimental value, so it has an associated error. Since the dissociation constant of water is (1.011 ± 0.005) × 10−14, pH of water at 25 °C would be 6.998 ± 0.001. The value is consistent, however, with neutral pH being 7.00 to two significant figures, which is near enough for most people to assume that it is exactly 7. The pH of water gets smaller with higher temperatures. For example, at 50 °C, pH of water is 6.55 ± 0.01. This means that a diluted solution is neutral at 50 °C when its pH is around 6.55 and that a pH of 7.00 is basic.

Most substances have a pH in the range 0 to 14, although extremely acidic or extremely basic substances may have pH less than 0 or greater than 14.

$$pH \text{ is } - \log_{10} [H+]$$
$$pH = - \log_{10} [H+]$$

or, by substitution,

$$pH = \frac{\varepsilon}{0.059}$$

The "pH" of any other substance may also be found (e.g. the potential of silver ions, or pAg+) by deriving a similar equation using the same process. These other equations for potentials will not be the same, however, as the number of moles of electrons transferred (n) will differ for the different reactions.

pH can be measured by addition of a pH indicator into the solution. The indicator color varies depending on the pH of the solution. Using indicators, qualitative determinations can be made with universal indicators that have broad color variability over a wide pH range and quantitative determinations can be made using indicators that have strong color variability over a small pH range. Extremely precise measurements can be made over a wide pH range using indicators that have multiple equilibriums in conjunction with spectrophotometric methods to determine the relative abundance of each pH-dependent component that make up the color of solution, or by using a pH meter together with pH-selective electrodes (pH glass electrode, hydrogen electrode, quinhydrone electrode, ion sensitive field effect transistor and others).

pH paper, indicator paper that turns color corresponding to a pH on a color key is usually small strips of paper (or a continuous tape that can be torn) that has been soaked in an indicator solution, and is used for approximations.

As the pH scale is logarithmic, it doesn't start at zero. Thus the most acidic of liquids encountered can have a pH of as low as −5. The most alkaline typically has a pH of 14. [1, 8, 23]

FLASH POINT

The flash point of a flammable liquid is the lowest temperature at which it can form an ignitable mixture in air. At this temperature the vapor may cease to burn when the source of ignition is removed. A slightly higher temperature, the fire point, is defined as the temperature at which the vapor continues to burn after being ignited. Neither of these parameters are related to the temperatures of the ignition source or of the burning liquid, which are much higher. The flash point is often used as one descriptive characteristic of liquid fuel, but it is also used to describe liquids that are not used intentionally as fuels.

There are two basic types of flash point measurement: open cup and closed cup. In open cup devices the sample is contained in an open cup (hence the name) which is heated, and at intervals a flame is brought over the surface. The measured flash point will actually vary with the height of the flame above the liquid surface, and at sufficient height the measured flash point temperature will coincide with the fire point.

Closed cup testers, of which the Pensky-Martens closed cup is one example, are sealed with a lid through which the ignition source can be introduced periodically. The vapor above the liquid is assumed to be in reasonable equilibrium with the liquid. Closed cup testers give lower values for the flash point (typically 5-10 K) and are a better approximation to the temperature at which the vapor pressure reaches the Lower Flammable Limit (LFL).

The flash point is an experimental measurement rather than a fundamental physical parameter. The measured value will vary with equipment and test protocol variations, including temperature ramp rate (in automated testers); time allowed for the sample to equilibrate, sample volume and whether the sample is stirred. The testers and protocols are specified in standards such as DIN 51758, ASTM 93, and Determination of flash point: Closed cup equilibrium method (ISO 1523:2002). [1, 2, 6, 23]

BOILING POINT

The boiling point of a substance is the maximum temperature at which a liquid can remain a liquid. Adding a bit of heat energy (latent heat of vaporization) can convert the liquid into a gas. A pure liquid may change to a gas at temperatures below the boiling point through the process of evaporation. Any change of state from a liquid to a gas at boiling point is considered vaporization. However, evaporation is a surface phenomenon, in which only molecules located near the gas/liquid surface could evaporate. Boiling on the other hand is a bulk process, so at the boiling point molecules anywhere in the liquid may be vaporized, resulting in the formation of vapor bubbles. A somewhat clearer (and perhaps more useful) definition of boiling point is *the temperature at which the vapor pressure of the liquid equals the atmospheric pressure.*

A saturated liquid contains as much thermal energy as it can without boiling (or conversely a saturated vapor contains as little thermal energy as it can without condensing). Saturation temperature means boiling point. The saturation temperature is the temperature for a corresponding saturation pressure at which a liquid boils into its vapor phase. The liquid can be said to be saturated with thermal energy. Any addition of thermal energy results in a phase change. If the pressure in a system remains constant (isobaric), a vapor at saturation temperature will begin to condense into its liquid phase as thermal energy (heat) is removed. Similarly, a liquid at saturation temperature and pressure will boil into its vapor phase as additional thermal energy is applied.

The boiling point corresponds to the temperature at which the vapor pressure of the substance equals the ambient pressure. Thus the boiling point is dependent on the pressure. Usually, boiling points are published with respect to standard pressure (101.325 kilopascals or 1 atm). At higher elevations, where the atmospheric pressure is much lower, the boiling point is also lower. The boiling point increases with increased ambient pressure up to the critical point, where the gas and liquid properties become identical. The boiling point cannot be increased beyond the critical point. Like wise, the boiling point decreases with decreasing ambient pressure until the triple point is reached. The boiling point cannot be reduced below the triple point.

If the Heat of Vaporization and the vapor pressure of a substance at a certain temperature is called, the normal boiling point (under standard pressure) can be calculated by:

$$T_B + \left(\frac{R(\ln(P_o) - \ln(101.325 kPa))}{\Delta H_{vap}} + \frac{1}{T_o}\right)^{-1}$$

Where **TB** is the boiling point under standard pressure, **R** is the ideal gas constant, **P0** is the vapor pressure at a given temperature, **T0** is that temperature, and **ΔHvap** is the heat of vaporization of the substance. Saturation Pressure, or vapor point, is the pressure for a corresponding saturation temperature at which a liquid boils into its vapor phase.

Saturation pressure and saturation temperature have a direct relationship: as saturation pressure is increased so is saturation temperature.
If the temperature in a system remains constant (an isothermal system), vapor at saturation pressure and temperature will begin to condense into its liquid phase as the system pressure is increased. Similarly, a liquid at saturation pressure and temperature will tend to flash into its vapor phase as system pressure is decreased. [1, 2, 3]

SURFACE TENSION

Surface tension is an effect within the surface layer of a liquid that causes that layer to behave as an elastic sheet. Surface tension is represented by the symbol σ, γ or T and is defined as the force along a line of unit length where the force is parallel to the surface but perpendicular to the line. Surface tension is measured in newtons per meter (N m-1), although the cgs unit of dynes per cm is normally used.

Surface tension can also be define by its thermodynamics, is work done per unit area. As such, in order to increase the surface area of a mass of liquid an amount, δA, a quantity of work, $\gamma \delta A$, is needed. Since mechanical systems try to find a state of minimum potential energy, a free droplet of liquid naturally assumes a spherical shape. This is because a sphere has the minimum surface area for a given volume. Therefore surface tension can be also measured in joules per square meter (J m-2), or, in the cgs system, ergs per cm2.

As stated above, the mechanical work needed to increase a surface is

$$dW = \gamma dA$$

For a reversible process,

$$dG = VdP + \gamma dA - SdT$$

therefore at constant temperature and pressure, surface tension equals Gibbs free energy per surface area:

$$\gamma = \left(\frac{\partial G}{\partial A}\right)_{P, T}$$

where **G** is Gibbs free energy and **A** is the area.
From the definition it is easy to understand that decreasing the surface area of a substance is always spontaneous ($\Delta G < 0$), on the contrary, in order to increase its surface a certain amount of energy is needed, as the process is,

per se, non-spontaneous (ΔG>0). A measure of how spontaneous (or non-spontaneous) is the change in the surface area is precisely the surface tension.

The definition of Gibbs free energy can be arranged to

$$H = G + TS$$

so partial derivation yields

$$\left(\frac{\partial H}{\partial A}\right)_P = \left(\frac{\partial G}{\partial A}\right)_P + T\left(\frac{\partial S}{\partial A}\right)_P$$

and applying the equations of state

$$\left(\frac{\partial G}{\partial T}\right)_{A,P} = -S$$

we obtain

$$\left(\frac{\partial \gamma}{\partial T}\right)_{A,P} = -S^a$$

where S^a means entropy per surface area.

Rearranging the previous expression Kelvin Equation I is obtained. It states that surface enthalpy or surface energy (different from surface free energy) depends both on surface tension and its derivative with temperature at constant pressure

$$H^a = \gamma - T\left(\frac{\partial \gamma}{\partial T}\right)_P$$

Surface tension depends on temperature; for that reason, when a value is given for the surface tension of an interface, temperature must be explicitly stated. The general trend is that surface tension decreases with the increase of temperature, reaching a value of 0 at the critical temperature.
 There are only empirical equations to relate surface tension and temperature:

$$\gamma V^{2/3} = k(T_c - T)$$

V is the molar volume of that substance
Tc is the critical temperature
k is a constant for each substance.
For example for water k = 1.03 erg/°C (103 nJ/K), V = 18 ml/mol and Tc = 374 °C.

Guggenheim-Katayama:

$$\gamma = \gamma^o \left(1 - \frac{T}{Tc}\right)^n$$

γ^o is a constant for each liquid and n is an empirical factor, whose value is 11/9 for organic liquids
Both take into account the fact that surface tension reaches 0 at the critical temperature.

Solutes can have different effects on surface tension depending on their structure:

- No effect, for example sugar
- Increase of surface tension, inorganic salts
- Decrease surface tension progressively, alcohols
- Decrease surface tension and, once a minimum is reached, no more effect: *surfactants*

$$\Gamma = \frac{-1}{RT} \left(\frac{\partial \gamma}{\partial \ln C}\right)_{T,P}$$

Gibbs isotherm states that:
Γ is known as surface concentration, it represents excess of solute per unit area of the surface over what would be present if the bulk concentration prevailed all the way to the surface. It has units of mol/m2
C is the concentration of the substance in the bulk solution.
R is the gas constant and T the temperature
Certain assumptions are taken in its deduction, therefore Gibbs isotherm can only be applied to ideal (very dilute) solutions with two components. [1, 3, 4, 5, 11, 23]
There are a number of instruments and methods used in determining surface tension the following are some examples:

Du Noüy Ring method: The traditional method used to measure surface or interfacial tension. Wetting properties of the surface or interface have little influence on this measuring technique. Maximum pull exerted on the ring by the surface is measured.

Wilhelmy plate method: A universal method especially suited to check surface tension over long time intervals. A vertical plate of known perimeter is attached to a balance, and the force due to wetting is measured.

Spinning drop method: This technique is ideal for measuring low interfacial tensions. The diameter of a drop within a heavy phase is measured while both are rotated.

Pendant drop method: Surface and interfacial tension can be measured by this technique, even at elevated temperatures and pressures. Geometry of a drop is analyzed optically.

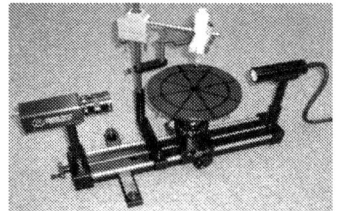

Ramé-hart goniometer

Bubble pressure method (Jaeger's method): A measurement technique for determining surface tension at short surface ages. Maximum pressure of each bubble is measured.

Drop volume method: A method for determining interfacial tension as a function of interface age. Liquid of one density is pumped into a second liquid of a different density and time between drops produced is measured.

Capillary rise method: The end of a capillary is immersed into the solution. The height at which the solution reaches inside the capillary is related to the surface tension by the previously discussed equation.

Stalagmometric method: A method of weighting and reading a drop of liquid. [3, 4, 5, 11]

SOLUBILITY

It is important for formulators to understand solubility. The term solubility indicates the maximum amount of solute (The substance present in the smaller proportion in a mixture) that can be dissolved in a given quality of solvent (The substance present in the largest proportion in a mixture) at a

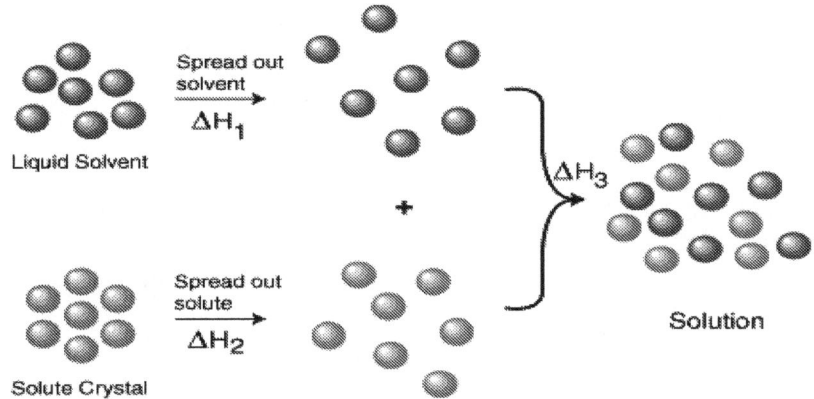

specific temperature. Solubility increases with increasing temperature, with a few exceptions.

Understanding the solubility of substances is extremely important in formulating products for both determining component ratios and minimizing costs of mixtures.

General rules of solubility are:

- All ammonium, potassium and sodium compounds are soluble in water.
- All acetates, chlorates and nitrates are soluble in water.
- All chlorides are soluble in water except those of silver, mercurous mercury, and lead.
- All sulfates are soluble in water except for those of barium and lead. Calcium, strontium, and silver sulfates are only slightly soluble.
- Carbonates, phosphates, oxides, silicates, sulfides, and sulfates are generally insoluble in water with the exception of ammonium, potassium, and sodium.
- All hydroxides are insoluble in water except for ammonium, potassium, sodium, barium, calcium, and strontium. Barium, calcium, and strontium are only slightly soluble in water.

Mixture concentrations can range from low concentrations to saturated concentrations (a saturated salt (NaCl) solution contains 35.7 grams of NaCl in every 100 mL of water) to supersaturated solutions for certain mixtures. An example of supersaturated solution is carbon dioxide gas in water. At the elevated pressure in the bottle, carbon dioxide can dissolve in water more than at atmospheric pressure. At atmospheric pressure, the carbon dioxide gas escapes very slowly from the supersaturated liquid. Supersaturated solutions of sugar and water are commonly used to make Rock candy. [1, 6, 23]

POLARITY

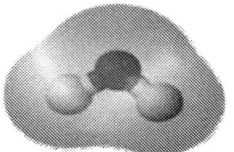
Water Molecule

Solvents and solutes can be broadly classified into polar (hydrophilic) and non-polar (lipophilic). The polarity can be measured as the dielectric constant or the dipole moment of a compound. The polarity of a solvent determines what type of compounds it is able to dissolve and with what other solvents or liquid compounds it is miscible.

A useful rule for predicting solubility is the term "Like dissolves like". This indicates that a solute will dissolve best in a solvent that has a similar polarity to itself. For example, strongly polar compounds like inorganic salts or sugars (e.g. sucrose) dissolve only in very polar solvents like water, while strongly non-polar compounds like oils or waxes dissolve only in very non-polar organic solvents like hexane. Solubility in water requires the resemblance to water, of which an important feature of water is the hydroxyl group (OH). Solvents which contain an OH or NH bond are identified as protic solvents. Hydrocarbons on the other hand are dissimilar to water because they are nonhydroxilic (no OH group) and are not solubility with water. These types of solvents are aprotic solvents. This is a of course a simplistic view, since it ignores many solvent-solute interactions, but it is a useful rule-of-thumb when developing a formulation especially at the initial screening process.

Synthetic chemists often use the different solubilities of compounds to separate and purify compounds from reaction mixtures. [1, 6, 23]

MISCIBILITY

Miscibility refers to the property of various substances, particularly liquids, that allows them to be mixed together and form a single homogeneous phase. For example, water and ethanol are miscible in all proportions. The solution of ethanol and water solute–solvent interaction hydrogen bonding force is comparable in magnitude to the attraction forces of the water molecules and ethanol molecules. By contrast, substances are immiscible if they cannot be mixed together such as oil and water.

In organic compounds, the length of the carbon chain often determines relative miscibility of the homologous series. For example, in the alcohols, ethanol has two carbon atoms and is miscible with water, whereas octanol has eight carbon atoms and is not miscible with water. Octanol's immiscibility is used as a standard for partition equilibria. This is also includes lipids, the very long carbon chains of lipids cause them to almost always be immiscible with water. [1, 6, 23]

EMULSIONS

An emulsion is a mixture of two immiscible (unblendable) substances. One substance (the dispersed phase) is dispersed in the other (the continuous phase). Examples of emulsions include butter and margarine, espresso, mayonnaise, along with many other products we use today. Many cleaning products are emulsions such as hand cleaners and creams.

Emulsions tend to have a cloudy appearance, because the many phase interfaces (the boundary between the phases is called the interface) scatter light that passes through the emulsion. Emulsions are unstable and thus do not form spontaneously. Energy input through shaking, stirring, homogenizers, or spray processes are needed to form an emulsion. Over time, emulsions tend to revert to the stable state of oil separated from water. Surface active substances (surfactants) can increase the kinetic stability of emulsions greatly so that, once formed, the emulsion does not change significantly over years of storage. For example, oil and vinegar salad dressing is an example of an unstable emulsion that will quickly separate unless mixed or shaken continuously.

There are three types of emulsion instability: flocculation, where the particles form clumps; creaming, where the particles concentrate towards the surface (or bottom, depending on the relative density of the two phases) of the mixture while staying separated; and breaking and coalescence where the particles coalesce and form a layer of liquid.

Emulsions are part of a more general class of two-phase systems of matter called colloids. Although the terms colloid and emulsion are sometimes used interchangeably, emulsion tends to imply that both the dispersed and the continuous phase are liquid.

SUBSTANCES AND MIXTURES

Substances are materials that have a defined composition and distinct property. Examples include water, citric acid, sugar, and iron just to name a few. These substances differ from one another in composition and have distinct properties that can be defined such as but not limited to color, texture, viscosity, and odor.

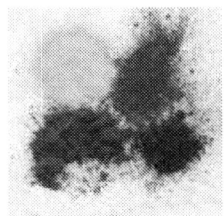  

Mixtures are a combination of two or more substances in which the components retain their properties. Examples of mixtures are chocolate mike, soft drinks, cement, and the many types of cleaning products use today. Mixtures do not have a constant composition that is why it is critical to implement and maintain a quality control process of the blending operation.

There are two types of mixtures: homogeneous and heterogeneous. A typical example of homogenous mixture is sugar and water. The sugar completely dissolves in the water creating a composition that is the same throughout the solution. In a heterogeneous mixture the individual components remain physically separate and require mechanical energy to maintain the mixture or an emulsifier which chemically binds the components together to maintain the mixture.

CHEMICAL COMPONENTS

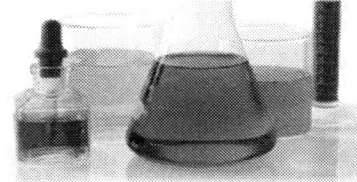

Industrial and household cleaning chemistry formulations contain a variety of chemicals including the basics such as, acids, bases, solvents, chelators, and surfactants. In order to develop a product, it is necessary for a formulator to have a solid understanding of the materials, function and characteristics.

ACIDS (mineral acids)

Acids are used in a variety of products such as metal cleaner, concrete cleaners, rest room products and even metal etchants. Understanding the fundamentals of acids helps in developing the right product for the right application. Acid are defined as substances that produce H+ ions in an aqueous solution.

Such as:

HCl (hydrochloric acid) aqueous → H+ (aq) + Cl-(aq)

HNO$_3$ (nitric acid) aqueous → H+ (aq) + NO$_3$-(aq)

Acids can also be defined as a substance that donates a proton to a solvent. When HCl dissolves in water a proton is donated to the solvent (the water)

HCl (aq) + H$_2$O (l) → H$_3$O+ (aq) + Cl-(aq)

in this instance the water acts like a base and accepts to proton from the acid.

Common Acids	
Name	Formula
Hydrochloric acid	HCl
Sulfuric acid	H2SO4
Nitric acid	HNO3
Phosphoric acid	H3PO4

Common properties of acids include:

- Sour taste
- Change litmus paper from blue to red (pH change)
- Nonoxidizing acids react with metals to produce hydrogen gas
- Reaction with carbonates to produce carbon dioxide [1,23]

Sulfuric Acid, H2SO4

Sulfuric acid is a strong mineral acid. It is soluble in water at all concentrations. Sulfuric acid has many applications, and is produced in greater amounts than any other chemical besides water. Principal uses include ore processing, fertilizer manufacturing, oil refining, wastewater processing, and chemical synthesis.

Although nearly 100% sulfuric acid can be made, this loses SO_3 at the boiling point to produce 98.3% acid. The 98% grade is more stable in storage, and is the usual form of what is described as concentrated sulfuric acid. Other concentrations are used for different purposes. Some common concentrations are:

**10% dilute sulfuric acid for laboratory use,
33.5% battery acid,
62.18% chamber or fertilizer acid,
77.67% tower or Glover acid,
98% concentrated acid.**

Different purities are also available. Technical grade H2SO4 is impure and often colored, but is suitable for making fertilizer. Pure grades such as US Pharmacopoeia (USP) grade are used for making pharmaceuticals and dyestuffs.

Polarity and conductivity

Anhydrous H2SO4 is a very polar liquid, with a dielectric constant of around 100.

$$2\ H_2SO_4 \rightleftharpoons H_3SO_4{+} + HSO_4{-}$$

This allows protons to be highly mobile in H2SO4. It also makes sulfuric acid an excellent solvent for many reactions. In fact, the equilibrium is more complex than shown above.

Reaction with water

The hydration reaction of sulfuric acid is highly exothermic. If water is added to concentrate sulfuric acid, it can boil and spit dangerously.

One should always add the acid to the water rather than the water to the acid.

Water is less dense than sulfuric acid and will tend to float above the acid. The reaction is best thought of as forming hydronium ions, by

$$H_2SO_4 + H_2O \rightarrow H_3O^+ + HSO_4^-,$$

and then

$$HSO_4^- + H_2O \rightarrow H_3O^+ + SO_4^{2-}$$

Because the hydration of sulfuric acid is thermodynamically favorable (ΔH = -880 kJ/mol).

Sulfuric acid is an excellent dehydrating agent, and is used to prepare many dried fruits. The affinity of sulfuric acid for water is sufficiently strong that it will remove hydrogen and oxygen atoms from other compounds; for example, mixing starch $(C_6H_{12}O_6)n$ and concentrated sulfuric acid will give elemental carbon and water which is absorbed by the sulfuric acid (which becomes slightly diluted):

$$(C_6H_{12}O_6)n \rightarrow 6C + 6H_2O$$

The effect of this can be seen when concentrated sulfuric acid is spilled on paper; the starch reacts to give a burned appearance, the carbon appears as soot would in a fire. A more dramatic illustration occurs when sulfuric acid is added to a tablespoon of white sugar in a cup and a tall rigid column of black porous carbon smelling strongly of caramel emerges from the cup.

Other reactions of sulfuric acid

As an acid, sulfuric acid reacts with most bases to give the corresponding sulfate. For example, copper(II) sulfate, the familiar blue salt of copper used for electroplating and as a fungicide, is prepared by the reaction of copper(II) oxide with sulfuric acid:

$$CuO + H_2SO_4 \rightarrow CuSO_4 + H_2O$$

Sulfuric acid can be used to displace weaker acids from their salts, for example sodium acetate gives acetic acid:

$$H_2SO_4 + CH_3COONa \rightarrow NaHSO_4 + CH_3COOH$$

Sulfuric acid reacts with most metals in a single displacement reaction to produce hydrogen gas and the metal sulfate. Dilute H2SO4 attacks iron, aluminum, zinc, manganese and nickel, but tin and copper require hot concentrated acid. Lead and tungsten are, however, resistant to sulfuric acid. The reaction with iron (shown) is typical for most of these metals, but the reaction with tin is unusual in that it produces sulfur dioxide rather than hydrogen. [1, 23]

Nitric Acid, HNO3

Nitric acid is an aqueous solution of hydrogen nitrate (anhydrous nitric acid). It is a highly corrosive and toxic acid that can cause severe burns. Colorless when pure, older samples tend to acquire a yellow cast due to the accumulation of oxides of nitrogen. If the solution contains more than 86% nitric acid, it is referred to as fuming nitric acid. Fuming nitric acid is characterized as white fuming nitric acid and red fuming nitric acid, depending on the amount of nitrogen dioxide present.

Pure anhydrous nitric acid (100%) is a colourless liquid with a density of 1522 kg/m³ which solidifies at -42°C to form white crystals and boils at 83°C. When boiling in light, even at room temperature, there is a partial decomposition with the formation of nitrogen dioxide following the reaction:

$$4HNO_3 \rightarrow 2H_2O + 4NO_2 + O_2 \text{ (72°C)}$$

which means that anhydrous nitric acid should be stored below 0°C to avoid decomposition. The nitrogen dioxide (NO2) remains dissolved in the nitric acid coloring it yellow or red at higher temperatures.

Nitric acid is miscible with water in all proportions and distillation gives an azeotrope with a concentration of 68% HNO3 and a boiling temperature of 120.5°C at 1 atm. Two solid hydrates are known; the monohydrate (HNO3·H2O) and the trihydrate (HNO3·3H2O).

Nitrogen oxides (NOx) are soluble in nitric acid and this property influences more or less, all the physical characteristics depending on the concentration of the oxides. These mainly include the vapor pressure above the liquid and the boiling temperature, as well as the color mentioned above.

Nitric acid is subject to thermal or light decomposition with increasing concentration and this may give rise to some non-negligible variations in the vapor pressure above the liquid because the nitrogen oxides produced dissolve partly or completely in the acid.

Nitric acid is a strong, monobasic acid, a powerful oxidizing agent which also nitrates many organic compounds and a monoprotic acid because there is only one dissociation.

Acidic properties

Nitric acid reacts with alkalis, basic oxides and carbonates to form salts, the most important of which is ammonium nitrate. Due to its oxidizing nature, nitric acid does not (with some exceptions) liberate hydrogen on reaction with metals and the resulting salts are usually in the higher oxidized state. For this reason, heavy corrosion can be expected and should be guarded against by the appropriate use of corrosion resistant metals or alloys.

Nitric acid is a strong acid with an acid dissociation constant (pKa) of −2: in aqueous solution, it completely ionizes into the nitrate ion NO_3^- and a hydrated proton, known as a hydronium ion, H_3O^+.

$$HNO_3 + H_2O \rightarrow H_3O^+ + NO_3^-$$

Reactions with metals

Being a powerful oxidizing agent, nitric acid reacts violently with many organic materials and the reactions may be explosive. Depending on the acid concentration, temperature and the reducing agent involved, the end products can be variable. Reaction takes place with all metals except the precious metal series and certain alloys.

As a general rule, oxidizing reactions occur primarily with the concentrated acid, favoring the formation of nitrogen dioxide (NO_2).

$$Cu + 4HNO_3 \rightarrow Cu(NO_3)_2 + 2NO_2 + 2H_2O$$

The acidic properties tend to dominate with dilute acid, coupled with the preferential formation of nitrogen oxide (NO).

$$3Cu + 8HNO_3 \rightarrow 3Cu(NO_3)_2 + 2NO + 4H_2O$$

Since nitric acid is an oxidizing agent, hydrogen (H) is rarely formed. Only magnesium (Mg) and calcium (Ca) react with cold, dilute nitric acid to give hydrogen:

$$Mg(s) + 2HNO_3\ (aq) \rightarrow Mg(NO_3)_2\ (aq) + H_2\ (g)$$

Passivation

Although chromium (Cr), iron (Fe) and aluminum (Al) readily dissolve in dilute nitric acid, the concentrated acid forms a metal oxide layer that protects the metal from further oxidation, which is called passivation.

Reactions with non-metals

Reaction with non-metallic elements, with the exception of silicon and halogen, usually oxidizes them to their highest oxidation states as acids with the formation of nitrogen dioxide for concentrated acid and nitrogen oxide for dilute acid. [1, 22, 23]

$$C + 4HNO_3 \rightarrow CO_2 + 4NO_2 + 2H_2O$$
or
$$3C + 4HNO_3 \rightarrow 3CO_2 + 4NO + 2H_2O.$$

Hydrochloric Acid, HCl

Hydrochloric acid is the aqueous (water-based) solution of hydrogen chloride gas (HCl). It is a strong acid, the major component of gastric acid and of wide industrial use. Hydrochloric acid must be handled with appropriate safety precautions because it is a highly corrosive liquid.

Hydrochloric acid or muriatic acid is an important industrial chemical for many applications, including the large-scale production of organic compounds, such as vinyl chloride for PVC plastic, and MDI/TDI for polyurethane, and smaller-scale applications, such as production of gelatin and other ingredients in food, and leather processing.

Hydrochloric acid (HCl) is a monoprotic acid, which means it can dissociate (i.e., ionize) only once to give up one H+ ion (a single proton). In aqueous hydrochloric acid, the H+ joins a water molecule to form a hydronium ion, H_3O^+.

$$HCl + H_2O \rightleftharpoons H_3O^+ + Cl^-$$

The other ion formed is Cl^-, the chloride ion. Hydrochloric acid can therefore be used to prepare salts called chlorides, such as sodium chloride. Hydrochloric acid is a strong acid, since it is fully dissociated in water.

Monoprotic acids have one acid dissociation constant, Ka, which indicates the level of dissociation in water. For a strong acid like HCl, the Ka is large.

When chloride salts such as NaCl are added to aqueous HCl they have practically no effect on pH, indicating that Cl− is an exceedingly weak conjugate base and that HCl is fully dissociated in aqueous solution. For intermediate to strong solutions of hydrochloric acid, the assumption that H+ molarity (a unit of concentration) equals HCl molarity is excellent, agreeing to four significant digits.

Of the seven common strong acids in chemistry, all of them inorganic, hydrochloric acid is the monoprotic acid least likely to undergo an interfering oxidation-reduction reaction. It is one of the least hazardous strong acids to handle; despite its acidity, it produces the less reactive and non-toxic chloride ion. Intermediate strength hydrochloric acid solutions are quite stable, maintaining their concentrations over time. These attributes, plus the fact that it is available as a pure reagent, mean that hydrochloric acid makes an excellent acidifying reagent and acid titrant (for determining the amount of an unknown quantity of base in titration). Strong acid titrants are useful because they give more distinct endpoints in a titration, making the titration more precise. Hydrochloric acid is frequently used in chemical analysis and to digest samples for analysis. Concentrated hydrochloric acid will dissolve some metals to form oxidized metal chlorides and hydrogen gas. It will produce metal chlorides from basic compounds such as calcium carbonate or copper(II) oxide. It is also used as a simple acid catalyst for some chemical reactions.

Hydrochloric acid is a strong inorganic acid that is used in many industrial processes. The application often determines the required product quality.

Regeneration of ion exchangers

An important application of high-quality hydrochloric acid is the regeneration of ion exchange resins. Cation exchange is widely used to remove ions such as Na+ and Ca2+ from aqueous solutions, producing demineralized water.

$$\text{Na+ is replaced by } H_3O+$$

$$\text{Ca}_{2}\text{+ is replaced by 2 } H_3O+$$

Ion exchangers and demineralized water are used in all chemical industries, drinking water production, and many food industries.

pH Control and neutralization

A very common application of hydrochloric acid is to regulate the basicity (pH) of solutions.

$$OH^- + HCl \rightarrow H_2O + Cl^-$$

In industry demanding purity (food, pharmaceutical, drinking water), high-quality hydrochloric acid is used to control the pH of process water streams. In less-demanding industry, technical-quality hydrochloric acid suffices for neutralizing waste streams and swimming pool treatment. [1, 22, 23]

Pickling of steel

Pickling is an essential step in metal surface treatment, to remove rust or iron oxide scale from iron or steel before subsequent processing, such as extrusion, rolling, galvanizing, and other techniques. Technical-quality HCl at typically 18% concentration is the most commonly-used pickling agent for the pickling of carbon steel grades.

$$Fe_2O_3 + Fe + 6\ HCl \rightarrow 3\ FeCl_2 + 3\ H_2O$$

In recent years, the steel pickling industry has developed hydrochloric acid regeneration processes, such as the spray roaster or the fluidized bed HCl regeneration process, which allow the recovery of HCl from spent pickling liquor. The most common regeneration process is the pyrohydrolysis process, applying the following formula:

$$4\ FeCl_2 + 4\ H_2O + O_2 \rightarrow 8\ HCl + 2\ Fe_2O_3$$

By recuperation of the spent acid, a closed acid loop is established. The ferric oxide by product of the regeneration process is a valuable by-product, used in a variety of secondary industries.
HCl is not a common pickling agent for stainless steel grades.

Production of inorganic compounds

Numerous products can be produced with hydrochloric acid in normal acid-base reactions, resulting in inorganic compounds. These include water treatment chemicals such as iron(III) chloride and polyaluminium chloride (PAC).

$$Fe_2O_3 + 6\ HCl \rightarrow 2\ FeCl_3 + 3\ H_2O$$

Both iron(III) chloride and PAC are used as flocculation and coagulation agents in wastewater treatment, drinking water production, and paper production.

Other inorganic compounds produced with hydrochloric acid include road application salt calcium chloride, nickel(II) chloride for electroplating, and zinc chloride for the galvanizing industry and battery production.

Production of organic compounds

The largest hydrochloric acid consumption is in the production of organic compounds such as vinyl chloride for PVC, and MDI and TDI for polyurethane. This is often captive use, consuming locally-produced hydrochloric acid that never actually reaches the open market. Other organic compounds produced with hydrochloric acid include bisphenol A for polycarbonate, activated carbon, and ascorbic acid, as well as numerous pharmaceutical products.

Other applications

Hydrochloric acid is a fundamental chemical, and as such it is used for a large number of small-scale applications, such as leather processing, household cleaning, and building construction. In addition, a way of stimulating oil production is by injecting hydrochloric acid into the rock formation of an oil well, dissolving a portion of the rock, and creating a large-pore structure.

Many chemical reactions involving hydrochloric acid are applied in the production of food, food ingredients, and food additives. Typical products include aspartame, fructose, citric acid, lysine, hydrolyzed (vegetable) protein as food enhancer, and in gelatin production. Food-grade (extra-pure) hydrochloric acid can be applied when needed for the final product.
[1, 22, 23]

Hydrofluoric Acid, HF

Hydrofluoric acid is a valued source of fluorine, being the precursor to numerous pharmaceuticals, diverse polymers and most other synthetic materials that contain fluorine. Hydrofluoric acid is best known to the public for its ability to dissolve glass by reacting with SiO_2, the major component of most glasses. This dissolution process can be described as follows:

$$SiO_2(s) + 4HF(aq) \rightarrow SiF_4(g) + 2H_2O(l)$$

$$SiO_2(s) + 6HF(aq) \rightarrow H_2[SiF_6](aq) + 2H_2O(l)$$

Because of its high reactivity toward glass, hydrofluoric acid is typically stored in polyethylene or Teflon containers. It is also unique in its ability to dissolve many metal and semimetal oxides. Because of its low tendency to dissociate into H+ and F- ions in water, it is properly considered a weak acid, but it is nonetheless *extremely corrosive*.

Hydrogen fluoride, compared with the other hydrohalic acids, is a weak acid in aqueous solution:

$$HF + H_2O \rightarrow H_3O+ + F-$$

When the concentration of HF approaches 100%, the acidity increases dramatically due to the following equilibrium:

$$2HF \rightarrow H+ + FHF-$$

The FHF− anion is stabilized by the very strong hydrogen - fluorine hydrogen bond. In acetic acid and similar solvents, hydrofluoric acid is the strongest of the hydrohalic acids.

Because of its ability to dissolve metal oxides, hydrofluoric acid is used in the purification of both aluminum and uranium. It is also used to etch glass, to remove surface oxides from silicon in the semiconductor industry, as a catalyst for the alkylation of iso-butane and butene in oil refineries, and to remove oxide impurities from stainless steel in a process called pickling. Recently it has even been used in car washes in "wheel cleaner" compounds. Hydrofluoric acid is also used in the synthesis of many fluorine-containing organic compounds, including Teflon and refrigerants such as Freon. [1, 22, 23]

Phosphoric Acid, H_3PO_4

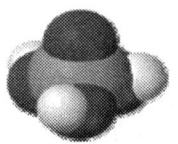

Phosphoric acid, also known as orthophosphoric acid is a mineral (inorganic) acid. Phosphoric acid molecules can combine with themselves to form a variety of compounds referred to as phosphoric acids in a more general way. The term "phosphoric acid" can also refer to a chemical or reagent consisting of phosphoric acids, usually mostly orthophosphoric acid.

Pure anhydrous phosphoric acid is a white solid that melts at 42.35 °C to form a colorless, viscous liquid.

Orthophosphoric acid is a non-toxic, inorganic, rather weak triprotic acid which, when pure, is a solid at room temperature and pressure. Orthophosphoric acid is a very polar molecule; therefore it is highly soluble in water. The oxidation state of phosphorus (P) in ortho- and other phosphoric acids is +5; the oxidation state of all the oxygens (O) is -2 and all the hydrogens (H) is +1. Triprotic means that an orthophosphoric acid molecule can dissociate up to three times, giving up an H+ each time, which typically combines with a water molecule, H2O, as shown in these reactions:

$$H_3PO_4(s) + H_2O(l) \rightleftharpoons H_3O^+ (aq) + H_2PO_4^- (aq)$$
$$H_2PO_4^- (aq) + H_2O(l) \rightleftharpoons H_3O^+ (aq) + HPO_4^{2-} (aq)$$
$$HPO_4^{2-} (aq) + H_2O(l) \rightleftharpoons H_3O^+ (aq) + PO_4^{3-} (aq)$$

The anion after the first dissociation, H2PO4-, is the dihydrogen phosphate anion. The anion after the second dissociation, HPO42-, is the hydrogen phosphate anion. The anion after the third dissociation, PO43-, is the phosphate or orthophosphate anion.

Because the triprotic dissociation of orthophosphoric acid, the fact that its conjugate bases (the phosphates mentioned above) cover a wide pH range, and because phosphoric acid/phosphate solutions are generally non-toxic, mixtures of these types of phosphates are often used as buffering agents or to make buffer solutions, where the desired pH depends on the proportions of the phosphates in the mixtures. Similarly, the non-toxic, anion salts of triprotic organic citric acid is also often used to make buffers.

Pure 75-85% aqueous solutions (the most common) are clear, colorless, odorless, non-volatile, rather viscous, syrupy liquids. Phosphoric acid is very commonly used as an aqueous solution of 85% phosphoric acid or H3PO4. Because it is a concentrated acid, an 85% solution can be corrosive, although not toxic when diluted. [22]

Rust removal

Phosphoric acid may be used by direct application to rusted iron, steel tools or surfaces to convert iron(III) oxide (rust) to a water soluble phosphate compound. Multiple applications of phosphoric acid may be required to remove all rust. The resultant black compound can provide further corrosion resistance (such protection is somewhat provided by the superficially similar Parkerizing and blued electrochemical conversion coating processes.) After application and removal of rust using phosphoric acid compounds, the metal should be oiled (if to be used bare, as in a tool) or appropriately painted, most durably by using a multiple coat process of primer, intermediate, and finish coats. [1, 22, 23]

ORGANIC ACIDS (carboxylic acids)

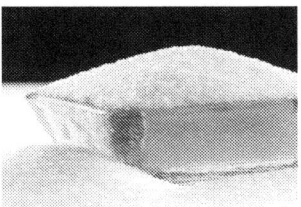

Organic acid is an organic compound that produces H+ ions in an aqueous solution. The most common organic acids are the carboxylic acids whose acidity is associated with their carboxyl group -COOH. Sulfonic acids, containing the group OSO3H, are relatively stronger acids. The relative stability of the conjugate base of the acid determines its acidity. Other groups can also confer acidity, usually weakly: -OH, -SH, enol group, and the phenol group. [1, 21, 23]

Common Organic Acids	
Name	**Formula**
Citric acid	$C_6H_8O_7$
Acetic acid	CH_3COOH
Sulfamic acid	H_3NO_3S
Oxalic acid	$C_2H_2O_4$
Malic acid	$C_4H_6O_5$

Acetic Acid, CH₃COOH

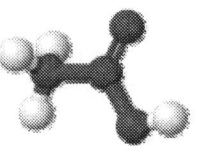

Acetic acid, also known as ethanoic acid, is an organic chemical compound best recognized for giving vinegar its sour taste and pungent smell. Pure, water-free acetic acid (glacial acetic acid) is a colorless liquid that attracts water from the environment (hygroscopy), and freezes below 16.7°C (62°F) to a colorless crystalline solid.

Acetic acid is corrosive, and its vapor causes irritation to the eyes, a dry and burning nose, sore throat and congestion to the lungs, however, it is considered a weak acid due to its limited ability to dissociate in aqueous solutions.

Acetic acid is one of the simplest carboxylic acids (the second-simplest, next to formic acid). It is an important chemical reagent and industrial chemical that is used in the production of polyethylene terephthalate mainly used in soft drink bottles; cellulose acetate, mainly for photographic film; and polyvinyl acetate for wood glue, as well as many synthetic fibers and fabrics. In households diluted acetic acid is often used in descaling agents. [1, 23]

Adipic Acid, $C_6H_{10}O_4$

Adipic acid is a carboxylic acid. It is a white crystalline powder appearing as an acid in aqueous circumstances, though it is not highly soluble. Adipic acid is as monomer for the production of nylon by a polycondensation reaction with hexamethylene diamine forming 6,6-nylon, the most common form of nylon. [1, 23] Other uses include:

> Monomer for production of Polyurethane
> Reactant to form plasticizers and lubricant components
> Food Ingredient as a flavorant and gelling aid

Citric Acid, $C_6H_8O_7$

Citric acid is a weak organic acid found in citrus fruits. It is a natural preservative and is also used to add an acidic (sour) taste to foods and soft drinks. It also serves as an environmentally benign cleaning agent and acts as an antioxidant. Citric acid exists in a variety of fruits and vegetables, but it is most concentrated in lemons and limes, where it can comprise as much as 8% of the dry weight of the fruit.

At room temperature, citric acid is a white crystalline powder. It can exist either in an anhydrous (water-free) form, or as a monohydrate that contains one water molecule for every molecule of citric acid. The anhydrous form crystallizes from hot water, while the monohydrate forms when citric acid is crystallized from cold water. The monohydrate can be converted to the anhydrous form by heating it above 74 °C. Citric acid also dissolves in absolute (anhydrous) ethanol (76 parts of citric acid per 100 parts of ethanol) at 15 degrees Celsius. Chemically, citric acid shares the properties of other carboxylic acids. When heated above 175 °C, it decomposes through the loss of carbon dioxide and water. [1, 23]

Food additive

As a food additive, citric acid is used as a flavoring and preservative in food and beverages, especially soft drinks. Citrate salts of various metals are used to deliver those minerals in a biologically available form in many dietary supplements. The buffering properties of citrates are used to control pH in household cleaners and pharmaceuticals.

Water softening

Citric acid's ability to chelate metals makes it useful in soaps and laundry detergents. By chelating the metals in hard water, it lets these cleaners produce foam and work better without need for water softening. Similarly, citric acid is used to regenerate the ion exchange materials used in water softeners by stripping off the accumulated metal ions as citrate complexes. [1, 22, 23]

Gluconic Acid, $C_6H_{12}O_7$

Gluconic acid is the carboxylic acid formed by the oxidation of the first carbon of glucose. When dissolved in water, it forms the gluconate ion $C_6H_{11}O_7-$; the salts of gluconic acid are also known as gluconates.

Gluconic acid occurs naturally in fruit, honey, kombucha tea and wine and is used as a food additive, an acidity regulator. It is also used in cleaning products where it helps cleaning up mineral deposits. It is a strong chelating agent, especially in alkaline solution. It chelates the cations of calcium, iron, aluminum, copper, and other heavy metals. [1, 22, 23]

Glycolic Acid, $C_2H_4O_3$

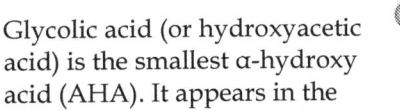

Glycolic acid (or hydroxyacetic acid) is the smallest α-hydroxy acid (AHA). It appears in the form of a colorless, odorless and hydroscopic crystalline solid that is highly soluble in water and related solvents. Glycolic acid is associated with sugar-crops and is isolated from sugarcane, sugar beets, pineapple, cantelope, and unripe grapes.

Glycolic acid finds applications in skin care products, most often as a chemical peel performed by a dermatologist in concentrations of 20%-80%

or at-home kits in lower concentrations of 10%. It is used to improve the skin's appearance and texture. It may reduce wrinkles, acne scarring, and hyperpigmentation and improve many other skin conditions. Once applied, glycolic acid reacts with the upper layer of the epidermis, weakening the binding properties of the lipids that hold the dead skin cells together. This allows the outer skin to "dissolve" revealing the underlying, healthier, smoother, brighter-looking skin.

Glycolic acid is also a useful intermediate for organic synthesis, in a range of reactions including: oxidation-reduction, esterification and long chain polymerization. It is used as a monomer in the preparation of polyglycolic acid and other biocompatible copolymers. Among other uses this compound finds employment in the textile industry as a dyeing and tanning agent, in food processing as a flavoring agent and as a preservative. Glycolic acid is often included into emulsion polymers, solvents and additives for ink and paint in order to improve flow properties and impart gloss. [1, 22, 23]

Oxalic Acid, $C_2H_2O_4$

Oxalic acid is t a relatively strong organic acid, being about 10,000 times stronger than acetic acid. The dianion, known as oxalate, is also a reducing agent and a ligand in coordination chemistry. Many metal ions form insoluble precipitates with oxalate, a prominent example being calcium oxalate, which is the primary constituent of the most common kind of kidney stone.

Oxalate is an excellent ligand for metal ions. It usually binds as a bidentate ligand forming a 5-membered MO_2C_2 ring. An example is potassium ferrioxalate, $K_3[Fe(C_2O_4)_3]$. The affinity of divalent metal ions is sometimes reflected in their tendency to form insoluble precipitates. Thus, oxalic acid also combines with metals such as calcium, iron, sodium, magnesium, and potassium in the body to form crystals of the corresponding oxalates, which irritate the gut and kidneys. Because it binds vital nutrients such as calcium, long-term consumption of foods high in oxalic acid can lead to nutrient deficiencies. [1, 22, 23]

Succinic Acid, HOOC–CH$_2$–CH$_2$–COOH

Succinic acid is a dicarboxylic acid. At room temperature, pure succinic acid is a solid that forms colorless, odorless crystals. It has a melting point of 185 °C and a boiling point of 235 °C. It is a diprotic acid. Esters of succinic acid are called dialkyl succinates. The acid is combustible and corrosive, capable of causing burns. [1, 23]

Sulfamic Acid, H_3NO_3S

Sulfamic acid, also known as amidosulfonic acid, amidosulfuric acid, aminosulfonic acid, and sulfamidic acid, is colorless, water-soluble compound that finds many applications. Sulfamic acid is used in the synthesis of compounds that taste sweet such as sodium cyclamate and related compounds as acesulfame potassium. Sulfamic acid is used as an acidic cleaning agent, typically for metals and ceramics. It is a replacement for hydrochloric acid for the removal of rust. In households, it is often found as a descaling agent in detergents used for removal of limescale.

Sulfamic acid is used in household chemical products such as Bar Keeper's Friend, some bleaches, and rust proofing treatments, also in wood restorers where the acid dissolves away a layer of dry surface wood to expose fresh material underneath including additives to automotive wheel cleaners, as a mordant in dyeing processes, as a rust remover in such applications as automotive shops and for the restoration of antiques, and as a recommended surface pretreatment for stainless steels (surface etch) before application of solid metal or polymer self-lubricating coatings. [1, 23]

Tartaric Acid, $C_4H_6O_6$

Tartaric acid is a white crystalline organic acid. It occurs naturally in many plants, particularly grapes, bananas, and tamarinds, and is one of the main acids found in wine. It is added to other foods to give a sour taste, and is used as an antioxidant. Salts of tartaric acid are known as tartrates. It is a dihydroxy derivative of dicarboxylic acid.

Important derivatives of tartaric acid include its salts, Cream of tartar (potassium bitartrate), Rochelle salt (potassium sodium tartrate, a mild laxative) and tartar emetic (antimony potassium tartrate).

Tartrate solutions can dissolve the layer of copper(II) oxide resulting in a Copper (II)-tartrate complex that results is easily soluble in water.

Tartaric acid may be most immediately recognizable to wine drinkers as the source of "wine diamonds," the small potassium bitartrate crystals that sometimes form spontaneously on the cork. These "tartrates" are harmless, despite sometimes being mistaken for broken glass, and are prevented in many wines through cold stabilization. The tartrates that remain on the inside of aging barrels were at one time a major industrial source of potassium bitartrate.
However, tartaric acid plays an important role chemically; lowering the pH of fermenting "must" to a level where many undesirable spoilage bacteria cannot live, and acting as a preservative after fermentation. In the mouth,

tartaric acid provides some of the tartness that is currently out of fashion in the wine world, although citric and malic acids also play a role. [1, 23]

BASES/ALKALI

Bases or alkalis are used in a variety of products such as, rest room cleaners, paint strippers, wax removers and pH buffering products. Understanding the fundamentals of bases and alkalis helps in developing the right product for the right application.

Bases are defined as substances that produce OH- ions in an aqueous solution. Such as:

NaOH (sodium hydroxide) aqueous → Na+ (aq) + OH-(aq)

KOH (potassium hydroxide) aqueous → K+ (aq) + OH-(aq)

Bases can also be defined as a substance that is capable of accepting a proton. Common properties of bases include: [1, 21, 23]

- Bitter taste
- Slippery texture
- Change litmus paper from red to blue (pH change)
- Similarly alkalis are base compounds with pH greater than 7 that dissolve in water. Alkalis are ionic salt of an alkali metal or alkaline earth metal.

Common Alkalis	
Name	Formula
Sodium Hydroxide	NaOH
Potassium Hydroxide	KOH
Potassium Carbonate	K_2CO_3
Ammonia	NH_3

Ammonia, NH_3

Ammonia is normally encountered as a gas with a characteristic pungent odor. Although ammonia contributes significantly to the nutritional needs of the planet, the gas itself is caustic and can cause serious health damage. Ammonia used commercially is usually named anhydrous ammonia. This term emphasizes the absence of water. Because NH_3 boils at -33 °C, the liquid must be stored under pressure or at low temperature. Its heat of vaporization is, however, sufficiently high that NH_3 can be readily handled in ordinary beakers in a fume hood. "household ammonia" or "ammonium hydroxide" is a solution of NH3 in water. The strength of such solutions is measured in units of Baume (density), with 26 degrees Baume (about 30 weight percent ammonia at 15.5 °C) being the typical high concentration commercial product. Household ammonia ranges in concentration from 5 to 10 weight percent ammonia.

Ammonium hydroxide is an aqueous solution of ammonia. Aqueous solutions of ammonia are sometimes referred to as ammonia water or aqua ammonia.

In aqueous solution, ammonia deprotonates some small fraction of the water to give ammonium and hydroxide ions according to the following equilibrium:

$$NH_3 + H_2O \leftrightarrow NH_4^+ + OH^-$$

With a base ionization constant (Kb) of 1.8×10-5, in a 1M ammonia solution about 0.42% of the ammonia will gain protons to become ammonium ions (equivalent to a pH of 11.63).

Aqueous ammonium hydroxide can also dissolve various metal oxides and hydroxides, such as copper(II) hydroxide to form ammine complexes. In such cases, the active agent is the ammonia, not the hydroxide salt. Solutions of ammonium hydroxide can also dissolve reactive metals such as aluminum and zinc, with the liberation of hydrogen gas. [1, 22, 23]

Sodium Hydroxide, NaOH

Sodium hydroxide also known as caustic soda or sodium hydrate is a caustic metallic base, which forms a strongly alkaline solution when dissolved in a solvent such as water. Caustic soda is widely used in many industries, mostly as a strong chemical base in the manufacture of pulp and paper, textiles, drinking water, soaps and detergents. Sodium hydroxide is also the most common base used in chemical laboratories, and it is also widely used as a drain cleaner.

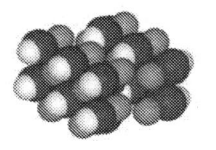

Sodium hydroxide is completely ionic, containing sodium ions and hydroxide ions. The hydroxide ion makes sodium hydroxide a strong base which reacts with acids to form water and the corresponding salts, e.g., with hydrochloric acid, sodium chloride is formed:

$$NaOH\ (aq) + HCl\ (aq) \rightarrow NaCl\ (aq) + H_2O\ (l)$$

In general such neutralization reactions are represented by one simple net ionic equation:

$$OH^- (aq) + H^+ (aq) \rightarrow H_2O$$

This type of reaction releases heat when a strong acid is used. Such acid-base reactions can also be used for titrations, and indeed this is a common way for measuring the concentration of acids. Related to this is the reaction of sodium hydroxide with acidic oxides.

Sodium hydroxide slowly reacts with glass to form sodium silicate, so glass joints and stopcocks exposed to NaOH have a tendency to "freeze". Flasks and glass-lined chemical reactors are damaged by long exposure to hot sodium hydroxide, and the glass becomes frosted. Sodium hydroxide does not attack iron or copper, but many other metals such as aluminum, zinc and titanium are attacked rapidly.

Many non-metals also react with sodium hydroxide, giving salts. For example phosphorus forms sodium hypophosphite, while silicon gives sodium silicate.
Unlike NaOH, the hydroxides of most metals are insoluble, and therefore sodium hydroxide can be used to precipitate metal hydroxides. One such hydroxide is aluminum hydroxide, used as a gelatinous floc to filter out particulate matter in water treatment.

Sodium hydroxide reacts readily with carboxylic acids to form their salts, and it is even a strong enough base to form salts with phenols. NaOH can also be used for the base-driven hydrolysis of esters (as is saponification), amides and alkyl halides. However, the limited solubility of NaOH in organic solvents means that the more soluble KOH is often preferred.

General applications

Sodium hydroxide is the principal strong base used in the chemical industry. In bulk it is most often handled as an aqueous solution, since solutions are cheaper and easier to handle. It is used to drive for chemical reactions and also for the neutralization of acidic materials. It can be used also as a neutralizing agent in petroleum refining.

Soap making (cold process soap, saponification) is the most traditional chemical process using sodium hydroxide.
Strong bases attack aluminum. This can be useful in etching through a resist or in converting a polished surface to a satin-like finish, but without

further passivation such as anodizing or allodizing the surface may become corroded, either under normal use or in severe atmospheric conditions.

Sodium hydroxide is used in the home as an agent for unblocking drains, provided as a dry crystal or as a thick liquid gel. The chemical mechanism employed is the conversion of grease to a form of soap, and so forming a water soluble form to be dissolved by flushing; also decomposing complex molecules such as the protein of hair. Such drain cleaners (and their acidic versions) are highly caustic and should be handled with care.

Chemical analysis

In analytical chemistry, sodium hydroxide solutions are often used to measure the concentration of acids by titration. Since NaOH is not a primary standard, solutions must first be standardized by titration against a standard such as KHP. Burettes exposed to NaOH should be rinsed out immediately after use to prevent "freezing" of the stopcock. Sodium hydroxide was traditionally used to test for cations in Qualitative Inorganic Analysis, as well as to provide alkaline media for some reactions that need it, such as the Biuret test. [1, 22, 23]

Potassium Hydroxide, KOH

Potassium hydroxide sometimes known as caustic potash and potassium hydrate is a metallic base. It is very alkaline and is a "strong base", as with sodium hydroxide.
It is a major industrial chemical used as a base in a wide variety of chemical processes. Some uses of KOH include acrylate ester copolymer coating, defoaming agents used in the manufacture of paper, saponifying oils for liquid soap, formulation aid for food, pH control agent, polyethylene resins, textile processing and as a catalyst in reactions like the production of biodiesel.

Other uses include industrial cleansers, washing powders, some denture cleaners, non-phosphate detergents, and drain or pipe cleaners.
A very significant use of KOH in terms of significance to the layperson is that alkaline batteries use an aqueous solution of KOH as an electrolyte. Thus, potassium hydroxide helps to power flashlights, smoke detectors, and other battery-powered household items, it is also an anisotropic etchant of silicon. [1, 23]

Potassium Carbonate, K_2CO_3

Potassium carbonate is a white salt, soluble in water (insoluble in alcohol), which forms a strongly alkaline solution. It can be made as the product of potassium hydroxide's absorbent reaction with carbon dioxide. It is deliquescent, often appearing a damp or wet solid. Potassium carbonate is used in the production of soap and glass.

Potassium carbonate is prepared commercially by the electrolysis of potassium chloride. The resulting potassium hydroxide is then carbonated using carbon dioxide to form potassium carbonate, which is often used to produce other potassium compounds.

$$2KOH + CO_2 \rightarrow K_2CO_3 + H_2O$$

Pearlash has been used for soap, glass, and china production. In the laboratory, it may be used as a mild drying agent where other drying agents such as calcium chloride may be incompatible. However, it is not suitable for acidic compounds. [1,23]

Sodium Carbonate, Na_2CO_3

Sodium carbonate also known as washing soda or soda ash is a sodium salt of carbonic acid. It most commonly occurs as a crystalline heptahydrate which readily effloresces to form a white powder, the monohydrate. It has a cooling alkaline taste, and can be extracted from the ashes of many plants. It is synthetically produced in large quantities from table salt in a process known as the Solvay process.

Sodium carbonate's most important use is in the chemical make-up of glass. When heated at very high temperatures, combined with sand (SiO_2) and calcium carbonate ($CaCO_3$), and cooled very rapidly, sodium carbonate can be used to form a transparent non-crystalline material, commonly known as glass.
Sodium carbonate is often used as an electrolyte in chemical applications. This is because electrolytes are usually salt based, and sodium carbonate acts as a very good conductor in the process of electrolysis.

Sodium carbonate is used as a water softener during laundry. It competes with the ions magnesium and calcium in hard water and prevents them from bonding with the detergent being used. Without using sodium carbonate, additional detergent is needed to soak up the magnesium and calcium ions. Sodium carbonate effectively removes oil, grease, and alcohol stains. Sodium Carbonate is also used as a descaling agent in boilers such as found in coffee pots, espresso machines, etc.

Sodium carbonate is widely used in photographic processes as a pH regulator to maintain stable alkaline conditions necessary for the action of the majority of developing agents.

Sodium carbonate is also used by the brick industry as a wetting agent to reduce the amount of water needed to extrude the clay, also a common additive in municipal pools used to neutralize the acidic effects of chlorine and raise pH.

In casting, sodium carbonate monohydrate is referred to as "bonding agent" and is used to allow wet alginate to adhere to gelled alginate.

Sodium carbonate is often used as a primary standard for acid-base titrations because it is solid and air-stable, making it easy to weigh accurately. [1, 22, 23]

BORAX

Borax, $Na_2B_4O_7 \cdot 10H_2O$

Borax is also called sodium borate, or sodium tetraborate, or disodium tetraborate, is an important boron compound, a mineral, and a salt of boric acid. It is usually a white powder consisting of soft colorless crystals that dissolve easily in water.

Borax has a wide variety of uses. It is a component of many detergents, cosmetics, and enamel glazes. It is also used to make buffer solutions in biochemistry, as a fire retardant, as an anti-fungal compound for fiberglass, as an insecticide, as a flux in metallurgy, and as a precursor for other boron compounds.

The term borax is used for a number of closely related minerals or chemical compounds that differ in their crystal water content, but usually refers to the decahydrate. Commercially sold borax is usually partially dehydrated.

A mixture of borax and ammonium chloride is used as a flux when welding iron and steel. It lowers the melting point of the unwanted iron oxide (scale), allowing it to run off. Borax is also used mixed with water as a flux when soldering jewelry metals such as gold or silver. It allows the molten solder to flow evenly over the joint in question. Borax is also a good flux for 'pre-tinning' tungsten with zinc - making the tungsten soft-solderable.

Other uses: component of detergents, component of cosmetics, ingredient in enamel glazes, component of glass, pottery, and ceramics, fire retardant, anti-fungal compound for fiberglass and cellulose insulation, component of slime insecticide to kill ants and fleas, sodium perborate monohydrate that is used in detergents, as well as for boric acid and other borates. [1, 22, 23]

CHLORIDE

The chloride ion is formed when the element chlorine picks up one electron to form an anion (negatively-charged ion) Cl^-. The salts of hydrochloric acid HCl contain chloride ions and can also be called chlorides. An example is table salt, which is sodium chloride with the chemical formula NaCl. In water, it dissolves into Na^+ and Cl^- ions.

Sodium Chloride, NaCl

Sodium chloride is also known as common salt, table salt, or halite. Sodium chloride is the salt most responsible for the salinity of the ocean and of the extracellular fluid of many multicellular organisms. As the main ingredient in edible salt, it is commonly used as a condiment and food preservative. Salt is currently produced by evaporation of seawater or brine from other sources, such as brine wells and salt lakes, and by mining rock salt, called halite. While most people are familiar with the many uses of salt in cooking, they might be unaware that salt is used in a plethora of applications, from manufacturing pulp and paper to setting dyes in textiles and fabric, to producing soaps and detergents.

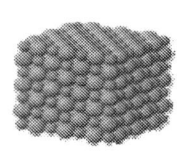

Salt is also the raw material used to produce chlorine which itself is required for the production of many modern materials including PVC and pesticides.
Industrially, elemental chlorine is usually produced by the electrolysis of sodium chloride dissolved in water. Along with chlorine, this chloralkali process yields hydrogen gas and sodium hydroxide, according to the chemical equation:

$$2NaCl + 2H_2O \rightarrow Cl_2 + H_2 + 2NaOH$$

Sodium metal is produced commercially through the electrolysis of liquid sodium chloride. This is done in a Down's cell in which sodium chloride is mixed with calcium chloride to lower the melting point below 700 °C. As calcium is more electropositive than sodium, no calcium will be formed at the cathode. This method is less expensive than the previous method of electrolyzing sodium hydroxide. [1, 23]

Ammonium Chloride, NH4Cl

Ammonium chloride in its pure form is a clear white water-soluble crystalline salt with a biting, slightly sour taste. The aqueous ammonium chloride solution is mildly acidic. Ammonium chloride is manufactured commercially by reacting ammonia, NH_3, with hydrogen chloride:

$$NH_3 + HCl \rightarrow NH_4Cl$$

It is sold in blocks at hardware stores for use in cleaning the tip of a soldering iron and can also be included in solder as flux. Other uses include a feed supplement for cattle, in hair shampoo, in textile printing, in the glue that bonds plywood, as an ingredient in nutritive media for yeast, in cleaning products, and as cough medicine. Its expectorant action is caused by irritative action on the bronchial mucosa. This causes the production of excess respiratory tract fluid which presumably is easier to cough up. It is the active ingredient in many antiperspirants, usually aerosols. It is also used in an oral acid loading test to diagnose distal renal tubular acidosis.
Ammonium chloride is used in snow treatment, namely on ski slopes at temperatures above 0 °C, to harden the snow and slow its melting. [1, 23]

Calcium Chloride, $CaCl_2$

Calcium chloride is an ionic compound of calcium and chlorine. It is highly soluble in water and it is deliquescent. It is a salt that is solid at room temperature, and it behaves as a typical ionic halide. It has several common applications such as brine for refrigeration plants, ice and dust control on roads, and in cement. It can be produced directly from limestone, but large amounts are also produced as a by-product of the Solvay process. Because of its hygroscopic nature, it must be kept in tightly-sealed containers

Because it is strongly hygroscopic, air or other gases may be channeled through a column of calcium chloride to remove moisture. In particular, calcium chloride is usually used to pack drying tubes to exclude atmospheric moisture from a reaction set-up while allowing gases to escape. It can also be added to liquids to remove suspended or dissolved water. In this capacity, it is known as a drying agent or desiccant. It is converted to brine as it absorbs the water or water vapor from the substance to be dried:

$$CaCl_2 + 2\ H_2O \rightarrow CaCl_2 \cdot 2H_2O$$

The dissolving process is highly exothermic and rapidly produces temperatures of around 60°C (140°F). This can result in burns if humans or other animals eat dry calcium chloride pellets. Aided by the intense heat evolved during its dissolution, calcium chloride is also used as an ice-melting compound. Unlike the more-common sodium chloride it is relatively harmless to plants and soil. It is also more effective at lower temperatures than sodium chloride. When distributed for this use, it usually takes the form of small white balls a few millimeters in diameter. It is used in concrete mixes to help speed up the initial setting. However, chloride ion leads to corrosion of steel rebar, so it should not be used in reinforced concrete. It is used for dust control on some highways, as its hygroscopic nature keeps a liquid layer on the surface of the roadway, which holds dust down. Calcium chloride tastes extremely salty and is used as an ingredient in some foods, especially pickles, to give a salty taste while not increasing the food's sodium content. It's also used as an ingredient in canned vegetables to maintain firmness. Used as an additive in plastics, used as a drainage aid for wastewater treatment. As an additive in fire extinguishers, in an additive to control scaffolding in blast furnaces, it can be used to make ersatz caviar from vegetable or fruit juices, it is used in Smartwater and some sports drinks as an Electrolyte, it is used to make fabric softener thinner, it is also used to treat certain electrolyte imbalances along with Calcium Gluconate. [1, 22, 23]

Potassium Chloride, KCl

Potassium Chloride is a metal halide composed of potassium and chlorine. In its pure state it is odorless. It has a white or colorless vitreous crystal, with a crystal structure that cleaves easily in three directions. Potassium chloride is also commonly known as "Muriate of Potash". Potash varies in color from pink or red to white depending on the mining and recovery process used. White potash, sometimes referred to as soluble potash, is usually higher in analysis and is used primarily for making liquid starter fertilizers. KCl is used in medicine, scientific applications and in food processing.

Potassium chloride can react as a source of chloride ion. As with any other soluble ionic chloride, it will precipitate insoluble chloride salts when added to a solution of an appropriate metal ion:

$$KCl(aq) + AgNO_3(aq) \rightarrow AgCl(s) + KNO_3(aq)$$

Although potassium is more electropositive than sodium, KCl can be reduced to the metal by reaction with metallic sodium at 850 °C because the potassium is removed by distillation.

$$KCl(l) + Na(l) \rightleftharpoons NaCl(l) + K(g)$$

This method is the main method for producing metallic potassium. Electrolysis (used for sodium) fails because of the high solubility of potassium in molten KCl.

As with other compounds containing potassium, KCl in powdered form gives a lilac flame test result.

The majority of the potassium chloride produced is used for making fertilizer, since the growth of many plants is limited by their potassium intake. As a chemical feedstock it is used for the manufacture of potassium hydroxide and potassium metal. It is also used in medicine, scientific applications, food processing, as a sodium-free substitute for table salt (sodium chloride). Potassium chloride t is sometimes used in water as a completion fluid in oil and gas operations. [1, 23]

Ferric Chloride, $FeCl_3$

Ferric chloride or iron(III) chloride is an industrial scale commodity chemical compound with many applications. The color of ferric chloride crystals depends on the viewing angle: by reflected light the crystals appear dark green, but by transmitted light they appear purple-red. Ferric chloride is deliquescent, fuming in moist air due to the evolution of HCl, which hydrates, giving a mist.
When dissolved in water, ferric chloride undergoes hydrolysis and gives off heat as the reaction is exothermic. The resulting brown, acidic, and corrosive solution is used as a coagulant in sewage treatment and drinking water production, and as an etchant for copper-based metals in printed circuit boards. Anhydrous ferric chloride is a fairly strong Lewis acid, and it is used as a catalyst in organic synthesis.

In industrial application, ferric chloride is used in sewage treatment and drinking water production, where $FeCl_3$ in slightly basic water reacts with the hydroxide ion to form a floc of iron(III) hydroxide, or more correctly formulated as FeO(OH)-, that can remove suspended materials.

$$Fe_3+ + 4\ OH- \rightarrow Fe(OH)_4- \rightarrow FeO(OH)_2-.H_2O$$

Another important application of ferric chloride is in the etching of copper in two-step redox reaction to copper(I) chloride and then to copper(II) chloride in the production of printed circuit boards.

$$FeCl_3 + Cu \rightarrow FeCl_2 + CuCl$$

$$FeCl_3 + CuCl \rightarrow FeCl_2 + CuCl_2$$

Ferric chloride is used as catalyst for the reaction of ethylene with chlorine, forming ethylene dichloride (1,2-dichloroethane), an important commodity chemical, which is mainly used for the industrial production of vinyl chloride, the monomer for making PVC. [1, 22, 23]

FLUORIDE, F

Fluoride is the ionic form of fluorine. Fluorides are organic and inorganic compounds containing the element fluorine. As a halogen, fluorine forms a monovalent ion (−1 charge). Fluoride forms a binary compound with another element or radical. Examples of fluoride compounds include hydrofluoric acid (HF), sodium fluoride (NaF) and calcium fluoride (CaF2).

Hydrofluoric acid is used in the etching of glass and other industrial applications, including integrated circuit manufacturing. Fluoride, as a concentrated gel, foam, or varnish, is used as a prescription drug. Fluoride ion has a very significant use in synthetic organic chemistry. The silicon-fluorine chemical bond is quite strong. Silyl ether protecting groups can be easily removed by the addition of fluoride ion.

Sodium fluoride or tetra-n-butylammonium fluorides (TBAF) are the most common reagents used. Sulfur hexafluoride is a nearly-inert, non-toxic propellant.

Fluorides are ingredients in such household products as cleaning solutions for metal, tile, brick, cement, wheels, radiators, siding, toilets, ovens and drains. Fluorides are also found in rust and water stain removers, silver solder and other welding fluxes, etching compounds, laundry sour, air conditioner coil cleaners and floor polishes. The fluorides that may be ingredients in these products and are potentially toxic are hydrofluoric acid ("HF"), ammonium bifluoride, ammonium fluoride, potassium bifluoride, sodium bifluoride, sodium fluoride and sodium fluosilicate.

The fluoride ion is systemically absorbed almost immediately. It is highly penetrating and reactive and can cause both systemic poisoning and tissue destruction. Fluoride ions, once separated from either HF or fluoride salts, penetrate deep into tissues, causing burning at sites deeper than the original exposure site. The process of tissue destruction can continue for days.
Fluoride absorption can produce hyperkalemia (elevated serum potassium), hypocalcemia (lowered serum calcium), hypomagnesemia (lowered serum magnesium), and metabolic and respiratory acidosis. These disturbances can then bring on cardiac arrhythmia, respiratory stimulation followed by respiratory depression, muscle spasms, convulsions, central nervous system ("CNS") depression, possible respiratory paralysis or cardiac failure, and death. Fluoride may also inhibit cellular respiration and glycolysis, alter membrane permeability and excitability, and cause neurotoxic and adverse GI effects. [1, 21, 23]
When exposure is through inhalation, fluorides can cause severe chemical burns to the respiratory system. Inhalation can result in difficulty breathing

(dyspnea), bronchospasms, chemical pneumonitis, pulmonary edema, airway obstruction, and tracheobronchitis. The severity of burns from dermal absorption can vary depending on the concentration of fluoride available, duration of the exposure, the surface area exposed, and the penetrability of the exposed tissue. [1, 22, 23]

NITRATE, N

Nitrates such as Ammonium Nitrate NH_4NO_3, Potassium nitrate KNO_3, and Sodium Nitrate $NaNO_3$ are commonly used in agriculture as a high-nitrogen fertilizer, and it has also been used as an oxidizing agent in explosives. Nitrate are used in metal cleaning compounds, etchants, and as glass refining agent and applied in TV glass motor, light glass. It is a useful chemical used as compound fertilizer and foliar spray. [1, 21, 23]

Ammonium Nitrate, NH_4NO_3

Ammonium nitrate is a white powder at room temperature and standard pressure. It is commonly used in agriculture as a high-nitrogen fertilizer, and it has also been used as an oxidizing agent in explosives, especially improvised explosive devices. The most common use of ammonium nitrate is in fertilizers. This is due to its high nitrogen content (a desirable feature of fertilizers as plants require nitrogen to make proteins) and inexpensive industrial manufacture.

Ammonium nitrate is also used in instant cold packs. In this use, ammonium nitrate is mixed with water in an endothermic reaction, which absorbs 26.2 kilojoules of heat per mole of reactant.

Products of Ammonium nitrate reactions are used in Airbags. Sodium azide (NaN_3) is the chemical used in airbags, as it decomposes to Na (s) and N_2 (g).

Ammonium nitrate is used in the treatment of some titanium ores and used in the preparation of nitrous oxide (N_2O):

$$NH_4NO_3(aq) \rightarrow N_2O(g) + 2H_2O(l)$$

Ammonium nitrate is used in survival kits mixed with zinc dust and ammonium chloride because it will ignite on contact with water. Ammonium nitrate can be used to make anhydrous ammonia, a chemical often used in the production of methamphetamine. [1, 22, 23]

Sodium Nitrate, $NaNO_3$

Sodium nitrate has long been used as an ingredient in fertilizers, explosives, and in solid rocket propellants, as well as in glass and pottery enamel, and as a food preservative (such as in hot dogs), and has been mined extensively for those purposes. Sodium nitrate, potassium nitrate, sodium sulfate and iodine are all obtained by the processing of caliche. Sodium nitrate is also synthesized industrially by neutralizing nitric acid with soda ash. Sodium nitrate was used extensively as a fertilizer and a raw material for the manufacture of gunpowder in the late nineteenth century. Sodium nitrate has antimicrobial properties when used as a food preservative. It is found naturally in leafy green vegetables. The presence of sodium nitrate in food is controversial due to the development of nitrosamines when the food, primarily bacon, is cooked at high temperatures. The nitrate compound itself is not harmful, however, and is among the antioxidants found in fresh vegetables. It can be used in the production of nitric acid by combining with sulfuric acid and subsequent separation through fractional distillation of the nitric acid, leaving behind a residue of sodium bisulfate. Less common applications include an oxidizer used in gunpowder, in blackpowder rockets, and as replacement for potassium nitrate. [1, 23]

PHOSPHATE

The phosphate ion carries a negative three formal charge and is the conjugate base of the hydrogen phosphate ion, $HPO_4^{(-2)}$, which is the conjugate base of H_2PO_4, the dihydrogen phosphate ion, which in turn is the conjugate base of H_3PO_4, phosphoric acid. Phosphate is also an organophosphorus compound with the formula $OP(OR)_3$.

Phosphate salts forms when a positively charged ion attaches to the negatively charged oxygen atoms of the ion, forming an ionic compound.

Many phosphates are insoluble in water at standard temperature and pressure, except for the alkali metal salts.
In dilute aqueous solution, phosphate exists in four forms. In strongly basic conditions, the phosphate ion ($PO_4^{(-3)}$) predominates, while in weakly basic conditions, the hydrogen phosphate ion ($HPO_4^{(-2)}$) is prevalent. In weakly acid conditions, the dihydrogen phosphate ion (H_2PO_4) is most common. In strongly acid conditions, aqueous phosphoric acid (H_3PO_4) is the main form.

Phosphates were once commonly used in laundry detergent in the form trisodium phosphate (TSP), but because of algae boom-bust cycles tied to emission of phosphates into watersheds, phosphate detergent usage is restricted in some areas.
Phosphates are used is a cleaning agents and degreasers, commonly used to prepare household surfaces for painting.

Phosphates can also be found as a food additive; it is used as an acidity regulator (buffering agent), emulsifier, thickening agent, nutrition enlargement agent and sequestrant (metal-chelating agent). [1, 22, 23]

Ammonium Phosphate, $(NH_4)_3PO_4$

Ammonium phosphate is obtained as a crystalline powder, on mixing concentrated solutions of ammonia and phosphoric acid, or on the addition of excess of ammonia to the acid phosphate $(NH_4)_2HPO_4$. It is soluble in water, and the aqueous solution on boiling loses ammonia and the acid phosphate $NH_4H_2PO_4$ is formed. Ammonium phosphate is used as an ingredient in some fertilizers as a high source of elemental nitrogen. [1, 22, 23]

Diammonium Hydrogen Phosphate, $(NH_4)_2HPO_4$

Diammonium hydrogen phosphate or diammonium phosphate is formed by evaporating a solution of phosphoric acid with excess of ammonia. It crystallizes in large transparent prisms, which melt on heating and decompose, leaving a residue of metaphosphoric acid (HPO_3). [1, 22, 23]

Ammonium Dihydrogen Phosphate, $NH_4 \cdot H_2PO_4$

Ammonium dihydrogen phosphate or monoammonium phosphate is formed when a solution of phosphoric acid is added to ammonia until the solution is distinctly acid. It crystallizes in quadratic prisms. Monoammonium phosphate is often used in the blending of dry agricultural fertilizers. It supplies soil with the elements nitrogen and phosphorus in a form which is usable by plants. The compound is also a component of the ABC powder in some dry powder fire extinguishers. [1, 22, 23]

SILICATE

Silicates are compounds that containing an anion in which one or more central silicon atoms are surrounded by electronegative ligands. This definition is broad enough to include species such as hexafluorosilicate ("fluorosilicate"), $[SiF_6]^{2-}$, but the silicate species that are encountered most often consist of silicon with oxygen as the ligand.

Silica, or silicon dioxide, SiO_2, is sometimes considered a silicate, although it is the special case with no negative charge and no need for counter-ions. Silica is found in nature as the mineral quartz, and its polymorphs.

Sodium Silicate, Na_2SiO_3

Sodium silicate also known as water glass or liquid glass, available in aqueous solution and in solid form, is a compound used in cements, passive fire protection, refractories, textile and lumber processing.

Sodium silicate is a white solid that is soluble in water, producing an alkaline solution. There are many kinds of this compound, including sodium orthosilicate, Na_4SiO_4; sodium metasilicate, Na_2SiO_3; sodium polysilicate, $(Na_2SiO_3)n$; sodium pyrosilicate, $Na_6Si_2O_7$, and others. All are glassy, colorless and dissolve in water. Sodium silicate is stable in neutral and alkaline solutions. In acidic solutions, the silicate ion reacts with hydrogen ions to form silicic acid, which when heated and roasted forms silica gel, a hard, glassy substance.
Sodium silicate is used, along with magnesium silicate, in muffler repair paste. When dissolved in water, both sodium silicate, and magnesium silicate form a thick paste that is easy to apply.

Concrete treated with a Sodium Silicate solution helps to significantly reduce porosity in most masonry products such as concrete, stucco, plasters. A chemical reaction occurs with the excess $Ca(OH)_2$ in the concrete that permanently binds the silicates with the surface making them far more wearable and water repellent. It is generally advised to apply only after initial cure has taken place (7 days or so depending on conditions). These coatings are known as silicate mineral paint. [1, 23]

SULFATE

Sulfate compounds arise when cations combine with the anion $SO_4(-2)$. Many sulfate salts are highly soluble in water. Exceptions include calcium sulfate, strontium sulfate, and barium sulfate, which are poorly soluble. The barium derivative is useful in the gravimetric analysis of sulfate: one adds a solution of, perhaps, barium chloride to a solution containing sulfate ions. The appearance of a white precipitate, which is barium sulfate, indicates that sulfate anions are present.

Sulfates are important in both the chemical industry and biological systems: Lead-acid battery typically uses sulfuric acid. Copper sulfate is a common algaecide. Magnesium sulfate, commonly known as Epsom salts, is used in therapeutic baths. Gypsum, the natural mineral form of hydrated calcium sulfate, is used to produce plaster. Sulfate compounds are used in many cleaning application and metal etching solutions. [1, 23]

Ammonium Sulfate, [NH4]2[SO4]

Ammonium sulfate is an inorganic chemical compound commonly used as a fertilizer. It contains 21% nitrogen as ammonia and 24% sulfur as sulfate. Its molecular formula is closely related to Mohr's salt an ammonium sulfate analogue with an iron atom within the compound.

Ammonium sulfate is not soluble in alcohol or liquid ammonia, but is highly hygroscopic and spontaneously absorbs water from the air at relative humidity > 81%. It is used largely as an artificial fertilizer for alkaline soils. In the soil the sulfate ion is released and forms sulfuric acid, lowering the pH balance of the soil (as do other sulfate compounds such as aluminum sulfate), while contributing essential nitrogen for plant growth. It is also used as an agricultural spray adjuvant for water soluble insecticides, herbicides, and fungicides. There it functions to bind iron and calcium cations that are present in both well water and plant cells. [1, 7, 21, 23]

Sodium Persulfate, $Na_2S_2O_8$

Sodium persulfate is a strong oxidizer and a severe irritant of skin, eyes, and respiratory system. It is almost non-hygroscopic and has particularly good ability to be stored for long time. It is easy and safe to handle. It is not combustible, but releases oxygen easily and assists combustion of other materials.

It is used as a bleach, both standalone (particularly in hair cosmetics) and as a detergent component. It is a replacement for ammonium persulfate in etching mixtures for zinc and printed circuit boards, and is used for pickling of copper and some other metals. It is a source of free radicals, making it useful as an initiator for e.g. emulsion polymerization reactions and for accelerated curing of low formaldehyde adhesives. It is also used as a soil conditioner and in manufacture of dyestuffs, modification of starch, bleach activator, desizing agent for oxidative desizing, etc.

Conditions/substances to avoid mixing persulfates with are: moisture, heat, flame, ignition sources, shock, friction, reducing agents, organic material, sodium peroxide, aluminum and powdered metals. [1, 23]

SOLVENTS

In most applications in industrial and household products the term solvent refers to a liquid that dissolves a solid or another liquid to create a new solution. The most common solvent use is water. Water is the base component in a majority of products; some cleaners are 90% water and only 10% active ingredients. In this section we will be focusing on solvents that are organic (carbon-containing) chemicals. These are called organic solvents. Organic solvents usually have a low boiling point and evaporate easily or can be removed by distillation. The following chart list the common names of organic solvent used in formulating clean products.

Organic Solvent Classes	
Name	Characteristic
Aliphatic solvents	Alkanes
Aromatic solvent	Benzene structure
Terpenes solvents	Isoprene base
Alcohols	Hydroxyl groups
Esters	Alkyl group Carboxylic acid
Halogenated solvents	Replaced H+ with Halide
Glycol ether esters	Alkyl ethers of ethylene glycol
Ketones	Carbonyl group (O=C) +2C
Glycols	2 (-OH groups)
Glycol ethers	Alkyl ethers of ethylene glycol
Amines	Organic derivative of ammonia

Aliphatic Solvents

Aliphatic solvents or alkanes are compounds that contain only one carbon-hydrogen and carbon-carbon single bond. The general formula is C_nH_{2n+2}, where the n in any integer. The simplest aliphatic compound is methane (CH_4 see figure on top). Aliphatics include not only the fatty acids and other derivatives of paraffin hydrocarbons, but also unsaturated compounds, such as ethylene, acetylene.

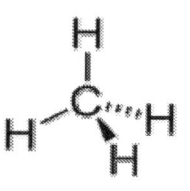

Aliphatic solvents are useful in dissolving many types of oils and varnishes. Determining the proper solvent to be used in a product is based on the physical characteristics of the solvent. Aliphatic solvents vary in evaporation rate, flash point, boiling range, along with other physical differences. Typically mixing experiments are required to determine the most effect solvent.

Common Aliphatic Solvents
140 Solvent
Heptane
Hexane
K-1 Kerosene
Lacquer Diluent
Mineral Spirits
Mineral Spirits, Rule 66
Naphtha
Odorless Mineral Spirits
PD-680A, Type I and II
Stoddard Solvent
VM&P Naphtha

Aromatic Solvents

Aromatic solves refer to compounds composed of benzene and its structural associations. An aromatic compound contains a set of covalently-bound atoms with specific characteristics:

1. A delocalized conjugated π system, most commonly an arrangement of alternating single and double bonds.

2. A coplanar structure, with all the contributing atoms in the same plane Contributing atoms arranged in one or more rings.

3. Special reactivity in organic reactions such as electrophilic aromatic substitution and nucleophilic aromatic substitution.

Aromatic molecules typically display enhanced chemical stability, compared to similar non-aromatic molecules. Aromatic molecules are able to interact with each other in so-called π-π stacking: the π systems form two parallel rings overlap in a "face-to-face" orientation. Aromatic molecules are also able to interact with each other in an "edge-to-face" orientation. Many of the earliest-known examples of aromatic compounds, such as benzene and toluene, have distinctive pleasant smells, this property led to the term "aromatic" for this class of compounds, and hence to "aromaticity" being the eventually-discovered electronic property of them. Aromatic solvents are useful in dissolving many types of oils and varnishes. Determining the proper solvent to be used in a product is based on the physical characteristics of the solvent. Aromatic solvents vary in evaporation rate, flash point, boiling range, along with other physical differences. Typically mixing experiments are required to determine the most effect solvent. [1, 21, 23]

Common Aromatic Solvents
Toluene
Ethyl Benzene
Xylene
HI-SOL 10 (Ashland chemical)
HI-SOL 70 (Ashland chemical)
HI-SOL 15 (Ashland chemical)

Terpene Solvents

Terpenes are organic solvents that are usually derived from natural sources such as pine trees or citrus fruit. They generally have strong characteristic odors. Terpenes have the molecular formula C_5H_8. The basic molecular formulas of terpenes are multiples of that; $(C_5H_8)n$ where n is the number of linked isoprene units. The isoprene units may be linked together "head to tail" to form linear chains or they may be arranged to form rings. As chains of isoprene units are built up, the resulting terpenes are classified sequentially by size as hemiterpenes, monoterpenes, sesquiterpenes, diterpenes, sesterterpenes, triterpenes, and tetraterpenes.

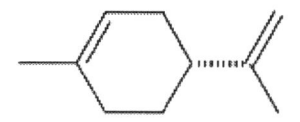

Specific terpenes used in cleaning are à-pinene, d-limonene (figure on the right), and turpentine, which is a mixture of terpenes. Terpenes are volatile organic compounds (VOCs) and are flammable or combustible.
Terpenes are good solvents for rosin fluxes, fingerprints, heavy petroleum greases, paint removers, adhesive residue cleaners, and a large number of hand cleaners. They can be used as a component of semi aqueous cleaning solutions or by themselves. Terpenes are strong solvents and are not compatible with some elastomers.
They can be used with immersion and ultrasonic systems, often working well at room temperature. Because terpenes may produce explosive mists when sprayed, they should only be used in spray applications with proper safety precautions, such as inert gas blanketing. [1, 21, 23]
In semi aqueous systems, the terpene can often be separated and reused. Terpenes are considered biodegradable, but should not be sent to the drain.

Alcohols

Methanol
also written
CH_3OH

Ethanol,
a 1° alcohol,
also written
CH_3CH_2OH

Isopropanol,
a 2° alcohol,
also written
$(CH_3)_2CHOH$

tert-Butanol
(2-Methyl-2-propanol),
a 3° alcohol, also
written $(CH_3)_3COH$

Alcohols contain a hydroxyl group (-OH). The general formula for a simple alcohol is $C_nH_{2n+1}OH$. The best know is Ethanol. Other forms of alcohol are usually described with a clarifying adjective, as in isopropyl alcohol (propan-2-ol) or wood alcohol (methyl alcohol, or methanol). The suffix -ol appears in the official chemical name of all alcohols.

Alcohols are in wide use in industrial and household products. Because of its low toxicity and ability to dissolve non-polar substances, ethanol is often used as a solvent in many cleaning products as well as in perfumes and in vegetable essences such as vanilla. Ethanol is often used as an antiseptic, to disinfect the skin before injections are given, often along with iodine. Ethanol-based soaps are now becoming commonplace within restaurants and are particularly convenient as they do not require drying due to the volatility of the compound. [1, 21, 23]

Esters

Esters are a class of chemical compounds and functional groups. Esters are formed in a condensation reaction between an alcohol and an acid in a reaction known as esterification. The most common type of esters are carboxylic acid esters (R1-C(=O)OR2), but other acids including phosphoric acid, sulfuric acid, nitric acid, or boric acid also form analogous esters. Volatile esters often have an odor and are found in perfumes, essential oils, and pheromones. Ethyl acetate and methyl acetate are used to produce, fatty acid esters and polyesters.

Ester	Characteristic odor or use
Bornyl acetate	**pine tree flavor**
Butyl butyrate	**pineapple**

Ethyl acetate	nail polish remover, model paint, model airplane glue
Ethyl butyrate	banana, pineapple, strawberry
Ethyl hexanoate	strawberry

Halogenated Solvents

Halogenated solvents are alkanes that have replaced one or more hydrogen atoms by a halogen atom. For example, when a mixture of methane and chloride is heated above 100°C methyl chloride is produced. The most important use of methyl chloride today is as a chemical intermediate in the production of silicone polymers. Smaller quantities are used as a solvent in the manufacture of butyl rubber and in petroleum refining. Methyl chloride is also used as a methylating and chlorinating agent in organic chemistry. It is also used in a variety of other fields: as an extractant for greases, oils and resins, as a propellant and blowing agent in polystyrene foam production, as an intermediate in drug manufacturing, as a catalyst carrier in low temperature polymerization, as a fluid for thermometric and thermostatic equipment and as a herbicide. [1, 23]

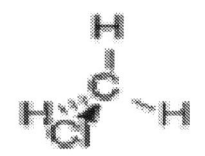

Halogenated Solvents
Methyl Chloride
Monochlorobenzene
Orthodichlorobenzene
Perchloroethylene
Trichloroethylene)

Glycol Ether Esters

Glycol ethers esters are acetates of glycols that have similar characteristics as glycol ethers. An acetate ester is an ester of acetic acid, with the general formula $C_2H_3O_2R$, where R is an organyl group. Acetate can also refer to cellulose acetate. Cellulose acetate can be found in many household products and as a component in some adhesives.

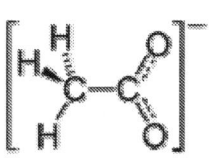

Glycol Ether Esters
Glycol Ether DB Acetate
Glycol Ether DE Acetate
Glycol Ether DPM Acetate
Glycol Ether EB Acetate
Glycol Ether PM Acetate

Ketones

A ketone is either the functional group characterized by a carbonyl group (O=C) linked to two other carbon atoms or a chemical compound that contains this functional group. A ketone can be generally represented by the formula: $R_1(CO)R_2$. The double-bond of the carbonyl group distinguishes ketones from alcohols and ethers. The simplest ketone is acetone. Acetone is a colorless, mobile, flammable liquid with melting point of −95.4 °C and boiling point of 56.53 °C. It has a relative density of 0.819 (at 0 °C). It is readily soluble in water, ethanol, ether, etc., and itself serves as an important solvent. The most familiar household use of acetone is as the active ingredient in nail polish remover. Acetone is also used to make plastic, fibers, drugs, and other chemicals.

Ketones
Acetone
Methyl Ethyl Ketone
Methyl Propyl Ketone
Methyl Isobutyl Ketone
Diacetone Alcohol

Glycols

Glycols are polymers of ethylene oxide or propylene oxide which can be represented by the general formula $HO(CH_2CH_2O)nH$ and $HO(CH_2CH_9CH_3)O)nH$, where n represents the average number of ethylene oxide and propylene oxide groups.

Glycols are linear polymers containing two terminal primary hydroxyl groups. The approximate average molecular weights of ethylene glycols are usually defined by the numbering system by the manufacturer.

Ethylene glycols are available in a range of molecular weights, usually from 200 to 8000 moles of ethylene oxide. The differences in the physical properties of the ethylene glycols are due to the molecular weights. As the molecular weight of the ethylene glycol increases, viscosity and freeze point increase, while solubility in water and organic liquids decreases. Ethylene glycols find utility in a variety of industries; the low odor and solvating power prove useful in many types of cleaning products. They also find application in lubricate bases for metalworking working and in textile application, also as mold release agents for ceramic and plastic, and as a component in adhesives, coating and inks.

Propylene glycols are available in a range of molecular weights, usually from 425 to 4000 moles of propylene oxide. The differences in the physical properties of the propylene glycols are due to the molecular weights. As the molecular weight of the propylene glycol increases, so does the viscosity, while solubility decreases

Propylene glycols function exceptionally well for synthetic lubricates and make them excellent defoamers and antifoams. [1, 23]

Glycols		
Product	L.B./GAL @ 20°C	Specific Gravity @ 20°C
Propylene Glycol	8.64	1.038
Ethylene Glycol	9.28	1.115
Hexylene Glycol	7.68	0.923
Dipropylene Glycol	8.51	1.023
Diethylene Glycol	9.31	1.119
Tripropylene Glycol	8.52	1.023
Triethylene Glycol	9.36	1.125

Glycol Ethers

Glycol ethers are produced by reacting an oxide with an alcohol (propylene oxide and ethylene oxide). Glycol ethers are colorless liquids with a mild odor. Most glycol ethers are miscible with water and our outstanding solvents and coupling agents because of their alcohol and ether characteristics.

Glycol ethers have a wide range of properties that are beneficial in industrial and household cleaners, metal cleaner, disinfectants, and germicides. The alcohol component of the glycol ether dissolves soluble soils while the ether component dissolves the oil soluble soil.
Glycol ethers can be used by themselves or in combination with surfactants to lower surface tension of aqueous cleaning solutions so that the cleaning agents are carried by the spreading water have an increased contact with the soil particulate.

Reduction in surface tension helps the cleaning agents to rapidly penetrate the soil particulate and lift the soil material from the surface being cleaned.

Glycol ethers are strong couplers, they work in combination with surfactants to pull oil and water soluble soil particulate from the surface or material being cleaned. Glycol ethers also keep the soil particulate suspended in solution and prevent it from redepositing on the cleaned surface.
Glycol ethers also contribute to the clarity of cleaning solutions. The water and cleaning components in solution sometimes produce a cloudy mixture. Glycol ethers added to this type of solution produce a clear product.

Glycol Ethers				
Chemical Name	Molecular wt	Flash Point °F	Surface tension (dynes/cm)	Solubility in water (ml/100ml)
Propylene Glycol Methyl Ether	90.1	90[1]	22.7	∞
Dipropylene Glycol Methyl Ether	148.2	167[1]	28.8	∞
Tripropylene Glycol Methyl Ether	206.3	232[1]	30.0	∞
Propylene Glycol n-Butyl Ether	132.2	138[2]	26.3	7.3
Dipropylene	190.3	212[1]	28.8	5.5

Glycol n-Butyl Ether				
Ethylene Glycol n-Butyl Ether	118.2	150²	27.4	∞
Diethylene Glycol Methyl Ether	120.1	197¹	34.8	∞

¹Setaflash
²Tag Closed Cup

Amines

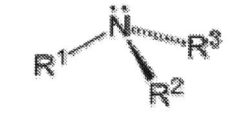

Amines are organic compounds and a type of functional group that contain nitrogen as the key atom. Amines are organic bases which are derivatives of ammonia in the same way that alcohols are derivatives of water. Structurally amines resemble ammonia, wherein one or more hydrogen atoms are replaced by organic substituents such as alkyl and aryl groups.

Amines have boiling point generally lower than the corresponding alcohols.

Methyl-, dimethyl-, trimethyl-, and ethylamine are gases under standard conditions, while diethylamine and triethylamine are liquids. Most other common alkyl amines are liquids; high molecular weight amines are solids. Gaseous amines possess a characteristic ammonia smell; liquid amines have a distinctive "fishy" smell.

Most aliphatic amines display some solubility in water, reflecting their ability to form hydrogen bonds. Solubility decreases with the increase in the number of carbon atoms, especially when the carbon atom number is greater than 6.

Aliphatic amines display significant solubility in organic solvents, especially polar organic solvents. Primary amines react with ketones such as acetone, and most amines are incompatible with chloroform and carbon tetrachloride.

The aromatic amines, such as aniline, have their lone pair electrons conjugated into the benzene ring, thus their tendency to engage in hydrogen bonding is diminished. Aromatic amines have boiling points are usually still high due to their larger size and diminished solubility in water, although they retain their solubility in suitable organic solvents only.

Amines have many uses in the industrial and household cleaning product along with dye application and medicine. Aqueous monoethanolamine (MEA), diglycolamine (DGA), diethanolamine (DEA), diisopropanolamine (DIPA) and methyldiethanolamine (MDEA) are widely used industrially for removing carbon dioxide (CO2) and hydrogen sulphide (H2S) from natural gas streams and refinery process streams. [1, 23]

Amines		
Product	L.B./GAL @ 20°C	Specific Gravity @ 20°C
Monoethanolamine	8.48	1.016
Triethanolamine	9.37	1.126
Diethanolamine	9.14	1.095
Morphline	8.36	1.004

SURFACTANTS

Surfactants are organic compounds that are amphiphilic, meaning they contain both hydrophobic groups (their "tails") and hydrophilic groups (their "heads").

Surfactants reduce the surface tension of water by adsorbing at the liquid-gas interface. They also reduce the interfacial tension between oil and water by adsorbing at the liquid-liquid interface. Many surfactants can also assemble in the bulk solution into aggregates. Some of these aggregates are known as micelles. The concentration at which surfactants begin to form micelles is known as the critical micelle concentration or CMC. When micelles form in water, their tails form a core that can encapsulate an oil droplet, and their (ionic/polar) heads form an outer shell that maintains favorable contact with water. When surfactants assemble in oil, the aggregate is referred to as a reverse micelle. In a reverse micelle, the heads are in the core and the tails maintain favorable contact with oil. Surfactants are also often classified into four primary groups; anionic, cationic, non-ionic, and zwitterionic (dual charge).

A surfactant can be classified by the presence of formally charged groups in its head. A nonionic surfactant has no charge groups in its head. The head of an ionic surfactant carries a net charge. If the charge is negative, the surfactant is more specifically called anionic; if the charge is positive, it is called cationic.

Some commonly encountered surfactants of each type include:

Anionic	based on sulfate, sulfonate or carboxylate anions
Sodium dodecyl sulfate (SDS)	ammonium lauryl sulfate, and other alkyl sulfate salts
Sodium laureth sulfate	sodium lauryl ether sulfate (SLES)
Alkyl benzene sulfonate	
Soaps, or fatty acid salts	
Cationic	based on quaternary ammonium cations
Cetylpyridinium chloride (CPC)	
Polyethoxylated tallow amine (POEA)	
Benzalkonium chloride (BAC)	

Benzethonium chloride (BZT)	
Zwitterionic (amphoteric)	
Dodecyl betaine	
Dodecyl dimethylamine oxide	
Nonionic	
Alkyl	Poly(ethylene oxide)
Copolymers	poly(ethylene oxide) and poly(propylene oxide)
Alkyl polyglucosides	
Octyl glucoside	
Decyl maltoside	
Fatty alcohols	
Cetyl alcohol	
Oleyl alcohol	
Octyl glucoside	
Cocamide MEA	
cocamide DEA	
cocamide TEA	

Cleaning

Detergency is the removal of a soil particulate from a substrate immersed in a medium usually through agitation in combination with a chemical that has the ability to lower the adhesion of the soil to the substrate, removing the soil and holding the material in suspension so that it can be washed away.

There are several mechanisms for removing soil. The three most common are suspension, roll-up, and emulsification. The mechanism used depends on the soil type, substrate, and washing parameters. The effectiveness of a particular surfactant will also depend on the se parameters.

Clay soils are cleaned by suspension. The clay soil materials are coated by the surfactant, detached from the substrate and held in suspension to prevent redeposition.

Roll-up and emulsification work best with oily materials. In aqueous solutions, if the surfactant displaces the oily substance for the substrate, droplets of oil will rise from the oil/substrate interface to the air/water interface. This displacement is termed roll-up. Roll-up does not occur in all detergency situations that involve oil. If the surfactant used is incapable of displacing the oil material from the substrate it can cause the oil to spread over the substrate in a thin film. Emulsification is required to clean the oil material.

In the laboratory cleaning/detergency is measured in many different ways. Methods for measuring detergency in hard surface cleaning, laundry, hand dishwashing, machine dishwashing, conveyerized machine washing and other applications have allowed formulators to correlate detergency with various surfactants properties. These properties include wetting, rewetting, foam generation, surface and interfacial tension, contact angle, micelle concentration, and HLB.

Surfactants very wildly in their detergency with different soil materials, selecting the proper surfactant is very important in cleaning formula generation. Typically the most effective surfactant detergency occurs at a 50% hydrophile and intermediate hydrophobes levels.

Dispersions

Dispersion is a system containing discrete particles or droplets in a second continuous phase. Dispersion is calculated by:

$$D = NS/NT$$

where D is the dispersion, NS is the number of surface atoms and NT is the total number of atoms of the material. Dispersion is an important concept in heterogeneous catalysis, since only atoms that are exposed to the surface are able to play a role in catalytic surface reactions. Dispersion increases with decreasing crystallite size and approaches unity at a crystallite diameter of about 1 nm.

The two classes of dispersions are suspensions, which solids are held in a liquid, and an elusion, liquids held within liquids. Dispersion can be created with agitation or surface modification. A stable dispersion results when the suspension or mixed materials remain separate or resist recombining. Usually when mixed solutions revert back to liquid-liquid state creaming, agglomeration or settling occurs.

When dispersed particles combined they may create flocculates or hard agglomerates. Flocculates have a feather or fluffy appearance and can easily be redispersed with minimal agitation. Hard agglomerates consist of dense, strongly bonded particles which form hard sediments.

Surfactants act as dispersants by means of two mechanisms. The first is electrostatic and the second is steric stabilization. In both systems the surfactant adsorbs on the particle surface creating a barrier between particles and reducing particle to particle interactions.

In highly polar media most particles carry a negative charge. Since cations have a positive charge they are adsorbed on the particles. This layer or ions is called the Stern layer. In the absence of surfactants the Stern layer is equivalent the shear plane. The change measured at the shear plane is called the zeta potential.

Electrostatic Stabilization

Electrostatic stabilization predicts that the higher charge level in the Stern layer results in a greater mutual repulsion of the particles. This repulsion prevents or inhibits flocculation. Adding the surfactant increases the zeta potential on the particles through hydrophobic-hydrophilic interactions. This causes repulsion and stabilizing the dispersion.

Steric Stabilization

In Steric stabilization nonionic surfactants are used to create a physical barrier that separates the particles. The hydrophobic portion adsorbs on the particle while the hydrophilic portion orients towards the bulk phase the surfactant inhibit aggregation by maintaining particle separation. Steric stabilization provides advantages over electrostatic stabilization such as:

- **Insensitive to changes in electrolytic concentration and pH**
- **Sediment redispereses easily**
- **Low viscosities are maintained**
- **Equally effective in aqueous and non aqueous solutions**

Foaming

In some application foaming is required for either performance or aesthetic reasons. It is important to be able to control the amount and stability of the foam generated.

Foam is a dispersion of air or other gases in a liquid in which the individual bubbles are separated by a thin liquid film. This film is called lamella. While the air or gas makes up a large portion of the foam, the foam's properties are determined by the properties of the thin film.

Pure liquids do not foam. Mixtures of compounds with similar polarities and functional groups also do not foam. Usually foam is created beneath the surface of the liquid by air or gas escaping from the liquid or by air or gas being introduced into the liquid. The foam can rapidly form a network of bubbles. Once the foam is created it may be either stable or unstable (flash foam). Since foam formation requires an increase of surface area, it also increases the free energy of the system. Since this is true then all foams are thermodynamically unstable. The foams stability depends on the rate of lamellae thinning and subsequent bubble rupture.

Several factors affect foam stability, viscosity of the surface film, surface elasticity and mobility. The Marangoni and Gibbs effect on foam stability propose that foams stabilize when the surface layers in the lamellae rapidly compensate for surface tension gradients that devolve from the disturbances as the foam ages. Surfactants can stabilize foam through one or more of the mechanisms.

Nonionic surfactants can produce stable, slow breaking foams; usually nonionic surfactants are identified as low to moderate foamers. Since nonionic surfactants are uncharged the foaming characteristics are not significantly affected by pH, but they do exhibit inverse solubility so the foaming properties are affected by temperature. Typically the nonionic surfactants produce foam until the temperature level reaches the cloud point, and then the foam level produced drops sharply or to some minimum level.

Gel Formation

Formulations of products in gel form are usually for aesthetics, convenience and functionality. Clear gels indicate purity and mildness. Gels also indicate concentrated performance.

A gel is a two phase colloidal system consisting of a solid and a liquid. Gels formulated with nonionic surfactants are generally made by cooling the solution after it has been heated to temperature; also some surfactants are liquid below room temperatures so the cold method may be required. Typically surfactants gelling tendencies increase as ethyl oxide content and total molecular weight increases.

Solubilization

Many cleaning products are mixtures of oil-soluble and water soluble products. These products have functional and/or aesthetic properties unavailable in the separate components of the product.

Solubilized products are stable, isotropic and may be transparent or opalescent dispersions of oil-soluble or water soluble components. Solubilized products are generally continuous in one of the phases.

The product is solubilized if the co-mixture is transparent or opalescent regardless of the mixing system used. The product may be a colloidal dispersion of micelles or a micro-emulsion rather than a true solution.

The selection of surfactants to test as solubilizers can be minimized by understanding certain factors that influence the mechanisms in the mixture, such as the factors of structure and quality of oil to be solubilized and the structure and the degree of hydrophilicity of the surfactant. For optimum compatibility the surfactant structure should be matched to the structure of the material to be solubilized. An example would be alky phenol oxyethylates should be considered for aromatic compounds while surfactants with initiated ethylenediamine should be considered for oils containing amines groups.

Lubrication

Lubricants serve two basic functions, minimize friction and minimize wear. Lubricates minimized friction be and wear by separating the two surfaces that move past each other. There are two lubrication conditions- boundary lubrication (low speed) and hydrodynamic lubrication (high speed).

The boundary lubricant maintains the separation of the two surfaces by the viscosity or by the associatively bonding one or both surfaces. It is important to note that high viscosity is detrimental to hydrodynamic lubrication.

Hydrodynamic lubrication should have low viscosity properties. The surfactants should have low internal cohesiveness or resistance to shear. In truth frictional phenomena dynamics are complicated and in some applications high molecular weight material sometimes provide the required viscosities needed in reducing hydrodynamic friction.

Wetting

Wetting is the displacement of one fluid on the surface by another. The primary measurement to determine wettability is a contact angle measurement. This measures the angle between the surface and the surface of a liquid droplet on the surface. For example, a droplet would have a high contact angle, but a liquid spread on the surface would have a small one. The contact angle θ and the surface energies of the materials involved are related by the Young–Dupré equation:

$$\gamma_{SV} = \gamma_{SL} + \gamma_{LV} \cos\theta$$

where γ is the surface tension between two substances and **S**, **V**, and **L** correspond to the solid, vapor, and liquid substances in a contact angle experiment respectively. A contact angle of 90° or greater generally characterizes a surface as not-wettable, and one less than 90° means that the surface is wettable. In the context of water, a wettable surface may also be termed hydrophilic and a non-wettable surface hydrophobic. Superhydrophobic surfaces have contact angles greater than 150°, showing almost no contact between the liquid drop and the surface. This is sometimes referred to as the "Lotus effect". This characteristic of spreading out over a greater area is sometimes called 'wetting action' when discussing solders and soldering.
Wetting is often an important factor in the bonding (adherence) of two materials.

A wetting agent is any substance that increases the ability of water to displace air from a liquid or solid surface. Wetting agents can cause three different kinds of wetting effects: spreading, adhesion, and immersion.

Spreading wetting occurs spontaneously only if the spreading coefficient is positive. For a liquid spreading over any surface the spreading coefficient is calculated from the surface and interfacial tensions of the liquids and surfaces involved. If the surface is a solid then the spreading coefficient is measured by calculating the contact angle of the spreading liquid on the solid surface using the angle between the solid/liquid interface and the liquid/air interface.

Adhesion wetting is defined by how tightly a liquid adheres to a surface with which it was not previously in contact, while adhesional wetting is measured by how much energy or work is required to separate a liquid from the wetted surface. The wetting of liquid to liquid is measured by surface and interfacial tensions; if a solid surface is measured the contact angle is used.

Immersion wetting occurs when a material not in contact with a liquid is immersed in the liquid. The wetting is measured by the change in surface free energy per unit area as wetting occurs. Measuring the liquid to liquid wetting the surface free energy is determined by the surface tension of the liquid and the interfacial tension between the two liquids. With solid material the free energy is determined by the contact angle between the liquid and the solid.

On hard surfaces wetting can be determined by comparing the diameter of a test drop of the surfactant solution and the pure liquid material on the surface being tested. Superior wetting is indicated if the diameter is greater than 300% of the control solution.

Thickening

Thickeners are surfactants that contain at least two hydrophobes, separated by a hydrophile. In products where water or other hydrogen bonding solvent is used as the continuous phase, the hydrophobe-hydrophile-hydrophobe structure causes thickening as the hydrophobe at each end interact with the neighboring molecules. This interaction of the hydrophobes is comparable to micelle formation. The mixture created by the surfactants extends throughout the solution and can resist shear, raise viscosity and thickens the solution.

Most thickeners are alkyl or alkylphenol hydrophobes, since these types of surfactants can readily form micelles, the surfactants increase the viscosity of water at concentrations below 2%.

Controlled Dissolution

In certain products it is desirable to have a solid based product that dissolves slowly in water, allowing the controlled release of ingredients over a period of time. Usually solids dissolve rapidly in a solvent until the solubility level is reached. In highly ordered compounds that form in water such as liquid crystals and gels dissolve more slowly. In this type of product the dissolving rate is based on the ability of water to penetrate and disrupt the gel structure.

Block copolymers that form gels dissolve slowly even when the copolymers are combined with other rapidly dissolving materials. As the gels strength increase it becomes more difficult to disrupt the surfactant structure increasing the dissolving rate of the product.
Block copolymers with high ethylene oxide content and high molecular weight are effective at reducing the dissolution rate of the product.

EMULSIFICATION

An emulsion is a suspension of particles of one liquid in a second immiscible liquid. Suspensions with liquid particles smaller than 0.2µ are microemulsions.

There are two basic types of emulsions: oil in water (o/w) and water in oil (w/o). The substance identified last indicates the continuous phase. Oil/water form or water/oil form depends on the emulsifier selected. Typically emulsifiers that are more soluble in water than in oil produce o/w emulsion; emulsifiers that are more soluble in oil produce w/o emulsions.

The stability of an emulsion is affected by a number of factors other than the choice of emulsifier. These factors include the type of mixing, the order of addition of ingredients, the mixing speed, mixing time and temperature. The ratio between components is also a factor in creating a stable emulsion. Depending on the stability required an emulsion can be considered usable from minutes to years depending on the intended use. Shelf life testing is very important aspect in development of emulsion products.

Hydrophilic emulsifiers usually functions the best in o/w emulsions as lipophilic emulsifier will function the best in w/o emulsions. To help the formulator in choosing the best emulsifier most surfactants have an HLB value designation. This HLB value indicates the w/o or o/w emulsification properties of the surfactant.

HLB system rates the hydrophilic/lipophilic balance (HLB) of the surfactant. The HLB value determines the emulsification characteristic of nonionic surfactants. Surfactants with a lower HLB value are more lipophilic, while surfactants with higher HLB values are more hydrophilic.

The HLB values help formulators by reducing the number of surfactants to be evaluated for a given application. General characteristic for HLB values:

HLB value	Surfactant function
4-6	Water/oil emulsifier
7-9	Wetting agent
8-18	Oil/water emulsifier
13-15	Detergent
10-18	Solubilizer

In formulating an emulsion type product the most difficult element is making the proper choice of emulsifier. This can be a complicated task because there are over three thousand surfactants to select from. The formulator must also identify the characteristics of the emulsion to be developed, is the emulsion water in oil (w/o) or oil in water (o/w), how stable is the emulsion to be, what are you cost limits, is the alkaline, is the emulsion stable for a salt or electrolyte mixture. The formulator also needs to identify how the emulsion product is to be used. How compatible is the chemistry of the product with the equipment the product will be used on or with. Identifying these factors systematically eliminates or discards certain types or groups of emulsifiers.

The following is an example on using the HLB system. The formulator has been assigned a project to develop an emulsion product that contains mineral sprits, cotton seed oil and a polyglycol. After a number of test solutions the formulator determines that the optimum concentrations for the product are:

Chemical	**WT%**
Mineral Spirits	**30%**
Cottonseed oil	**50%**
Polyglycol	**20%**

The formulator then identifies the HLB value for each component:

Chemical	**HLB value**
Mineral Spirits	14
Cottonseed oil	6
Polyglycol	8

Calculation for the HLB emulsifier:

Mineral Spirits	30%	X	14	= 4.2
Cottonseed oil	50%	X	6	=3.0
Polyglycol	20%	X	8	=1.6
				8.8 HLB

Base on the HLB system the emulsifier or blend of emulsifiers having a HLB of 8.8 will make a stable emulsion with these ingredients. Now this doe not mean that every emulsifier with an 8.8 HLB will work. The emulsifier requires the right chemical family and proper mixing order, and mixing speed. Remember that different suppliers and even batches of materials vary which can result in variation in HLB required to emulsify the ingredients.

The HLB system was designed for nonionic surfactants with hydrocarbon lipophiles. Variations are found in HLB values from different hydrocarbon lipophiles, the HLB values of EO/PO copolymers do not correlate exactly with HLB values for EO/hydrocarbon surfactants. [1, 6, 21, 23]

SURFACTANT TYPES AND APPLICATION

Surfactants play a major role in industrial and household cleaning products; they provide the wetting, foaming, emulsification, dispersion, detergency, and viscosity, antistreaking, defoaming properties necessary in developing a wide range of products from laundry products, industrial, institutional, household, health care, metal cleaning, and emulsions.

The formulator must be able to identify which surfactant or surfactants are required to provide the performance needed in the product to be developed. There are thousands of surfactants to choose from, so it is imperative that the formulator understand the different types and characteristics of surfactants in order to develop a product to address the customer's needs.

Surfactants are divided into five basic groups: ***Amphoteric***, ***Anionic***, ***Cationic***, ***Nonionic***, and ***Specialty*** surfactants.

This section's focus is to identify general types of surfactants formulators use and describes the applications of these materials. This is a general overview and does not include every type of surfactant possible; this would be beyond the scope of this book.

AMPHOTERIC SURFACTANTS

Amphoteric surfactants possess both anionic and cationic charges. Generally they behave anionic in alkaline conditions and cationic in acid media. Amphoteric surfactants maintain their compatibility with all anionic, cationic and nonionic solutions in any pH. Amphoterics are used because of their low skin and eye irritation and the ability to mollify the irritation characteristics of other surfactants. Amphoterics have the following characteristics:

Excellent foaming, emulsifying and wetting properties
Stable in strong acids and alkali
Hydroliticaly stable
Synergistic with nonionics
Stable to quaternary germicides
Used in hard surface detergents
Non toxic
Biodegradable
Mild to skin and eyes

Amphoterics and Applications

Disodium Lauroampho Diacetate
Derived from lauric acid, it has high foaming in greasy soils and is used in shampoos and degreasers.

Disodium Cocoampho Diacetate
Functions as mild emulsifiers and solubilizers, used with foaming and cleaning agents to reduce the irritation of other surfactants. Used in mild shampoos, skin cleansers; make up removers and other pharmaceuticals.

Sodium Lauroampho Acetate
Used for personal care products and Household, Institutional and Industrial cleaners and burnishing compounds.

Disodium Capryloampho Diacetate
This is a low foaming surfactant which has excellent wetting and is stable in strong acids and bases. Used in steam and spray metal cleaners.

Sodium Amphocarboxylate
This is a low foaming surfactant which is stable in caustic soda (sodium hydroxide) non-discoloring on caustic and stable in strong acids. It demonstrates excellent wetting properties. Used in bottle washing, alkaline degreasing, wax strippers, and mercerizing. This surfactants in also used in food plant and preparation areas.

Sodium Cocoampho Acetate

Functions as mild emulsifiers and solubilizers, used with foaming and cleaning agents to reduce the irritation of other surfactants. Used in mild shampoos, skin cleansers; make up removers and other pharmaceuticals

Sodium Cocoampho Propionate

Widely used in heavy duty industrial cleaners, with a high electrolyte tolerance.

Disodium Cocoampho Dipropionate

This is used as a mild emulsifier, solubilizers and in foaming and cleaning agents. This is also used to reduce irritation from other surfactants.

Sodium Capryloampho Propionate

This is used as a low foaming agent which is stable in strong acids and bases and has effective rust inhibiting properties.

Disodium Capryloampho Dipropionate

This is a low foaming surfactant which has excellent wetting and is stable in strong acids and bases. Used in steam and spray metal cleaners.

Sodium Cocoampho Hydroxypropyl Sulfonate

This is an excellent detergent with wetting, solubilizing characteristics and exhibits corrosion inhibitor properties in acid cleaners, aluminum cleaners, and in pickling applications. This is also used in fabric washes and metal polishes.

Lauramidopropyl Betaine

Has excellent foaming characteristics over the entire pH range.

Coco/Oleamidopropyl Betaine

This is used as a foaming enhancer and viscosity builder.

Oleamidopropyl Betaine

This is used as a conditioning and detangling agent for shampoos with excellent viscosity building properties for bath gels and gel shampoos.

Cocamidopropyl Betaine

This is used as a foam booster, foaming agent, thickener and conditioning agent. This surfactant provides performance booster in shampoos, bubble baths, and skin cleansers. It also provides irritation mollifying agents for baby shampoos and ultra mild personal car products.

Alkylether Hydroxypropyl Sultaine

This is a non foaming wetting agent which is soluble and compatible in 50% caustic soda (sodium hydroxide) and high acid level solutions.

Cocamidopropyl Hydroxy Sultaine
This surfactant is a high foaming product over a wide pH and water hardness range. It forms clear solutions with cationics and is used in shampoos and bath products. It is also used in oil drill applications.

Sodium Laurimino Dipropionate
This is used in hard surface detergency application; it has moderate foaming, corrosion inhibition, antistatic and lubrication properties.

Dihydroxyethyl Tallow Glycinate
This surfactant has the ability to thicken hydrochloric acid solutions and provide excellent stability in acid and alkaline systems.

ANIONIC SURFACTANTS

Anionic surfactants carry a negative charge on the hydrophilic part of the surfactant, typically in the form of a carboxylate such as a phosphate, sulfate or Sulfonate radical. Anionic surfactants have a wide range of applications including emulsion polymerization, agro chemicals, personal care products, household and industrial cleaners. Anionic surfactant can function as emulsifiers, wetting agents, foaming and frothing agents for multiple types of washes and cleaners.

Anionics and Applications

Ammonium Lauryl Sulfate
This surfactant is used for high foaming products for low pH cleaners and cosmetics. It can also produce high viscosity liquids and gels.

Magnesium Lauryl Sulfate
This surfactant is used to produce cleaners and bath products for low temperature clarity requirements; this is used for foam carpet cleaning and upholstery cleaners.

Sodium2-Ethylhexyl Sulfate
This surfactant demonstrates excellent wetting properties with low foaming, coupling and alkaline stability.

Sodium Cetyl Sulfate
This surfactant is used for emulsifying with polymerization and post stabilization. It is also a softener and lubricate for cotton and rayon. The surfactant provides deep cleaning and lubrication to skin, scalp and hair care products.

Sodium Isodecyl Sulfate
This is a low foaming, rapid wetting surfactant which is stable to relatively high electrolyte levels.

Sodium Lauryl Sulfate
This surfactant has a low cloud point; it provides low temperature clarity with latex stability and particle size uniformity. It is also used in polymerization, in bath and shampoos, pre-pearlization.

Sodium Octyl Sulfate
This surfactant provides rapid wetting and low foam for metal cleaners, rinse aides and textile mercerizing.

Sodium Oleyl Sulfate
This surfactant provides emolliency and mildness to skin and hair care products, it is extremely water soluble

Sodium Tridecyl Sulfate
This is surfactant is used in polymerization of PVC, styrene and acrylics and used in detergents.

Triethanolamine Lauryl Sulfate
This surfactant is a mild high foaming product used in shampoos and skin cleansers.

Ammonium Linear Alcohol ether Sulfate
This is a high foaming surfactant, highly effective in high electrolytic systems and produces stable foam. This is typically used as air entraining agent in concrete, foaming agent for light weight cements and gypsum wall board, also as a foaming agent for oil and gas wells.

Ammonium Laureth(2) Sulfate
This is used in shampoos, bubble bath products, skin cleansers and cosmetics.

Ammonium Nonylphenol Ether Sulfate
This is in high foaming application such as car washing and scrubbing soaps. It is also used for Ag chemicals and petroleum waxes as an emulsifier. It also has antistat applications for plastics and fibers.

Sodium Laureth Sulfate
This is used for high foaming shampoos, bath products, skin cleansers and hand soaps.

Ammonium Laureth Sulfate
This is a highly active product used in shampoos hand dishwashing and general detergent products.

Linear Calcium Dodecylbenzene Sulfonate
This is a biodegradable co-emulsifier for anionic and nonionic emulsifier blends. This is typically used in pesticide emulsion concentrate and in dye dispersant for polyester.

Isopropylamine Dodecylbenzene Sulfonate
This is an oil soluble emulsifier used in solvent degreasers, emulsion cleaners, dry cleaning soaps, oil and spill clean up applications. It can also be used to solubilize water in fuel oil to prevent corrosion.

Sodium Dodecylbenzene Sulfonate

This is a high purity emulsifier for polymerization of SBR, vinyl acetate, vinyl chloride, styrene and acrylic lattices. It is also used in a broad range of cleaners.

Sodium Alpha Olefin Sulfonate

This is a high foaming detergent and emulsifier, used in shampoos, bubble baths, liquid hand soaps, body soaps, dishwash and carwash applications. It is also used in pet shampoos and general cleaning formulations.

Disodium Dodecyl Diphenyl Oxide Disulfonate

This surfactant has a high charge density, which is stable at high levels of electrolytes and acids. It has good wetting properties and detergency with hydrotroping power. This is used as a leveling agent in dying nylon, solubilizing agent in phenolic sanitizers.

Sodium Dibutyl Naphthalene Sulfonate
Sodium Diisopropyl Naphthalene Sulfonate

These are used as an effective dispersants for pigments, clays and dyes, wettable powders, Latex and inks. These are also used in leather dyes, leveling and wetting. In textiles these surfactants are used for wetting and dispersing and penetrating agents. In cotton and rayon application are used as wetting agents.

Disodium Lauramide (MEA) Sulfosuccinate

This surfactant functions with cationics, it improves flash foam and has the ability to dry to a brittle tack free residue used in carpet cleaners.

Disodium Laureth (3) Sulfosuccinate

This is an exceptionally mild surfactant with good flash foam characteristics. It is used in bath gels, bubble bath and body care products.

Disodium Lauryl Sulfosuccinate

This is a mild and high foaming surfactant used in shampoos, liquid soaps and fine fabric detergents.

Disodium Ricinoleamide (MEA) Sulfosuccinate

This is used as a counter irritant for anionic based products. It is used in shampoos, bubble bath, skin creams, make-up bases, shaving creams, cutting oils and car wash product.

Sodium Dinoyl Sulfosuccinate

This surfactant is used for wetting and penetrant in padding and long liquor dying, sizing and desizing. It is also used in rewetting for yarn and piece goods.

Sodium Dioctyl Sulfosuccinate

This is an excellent wetting and penetrating agent for textile processing. It is used as a dewatering agent for mineral processing and it is also used in dry cleaning, emulsion polymerization, wallpaper and battery separators. It is also used for rewetting in paper towels and tissue and dried kraft pulp and paper making felts.

Disodium N-Alkyl Sulfosuccinamate

This is used as an effective foaming agent and foam stabilizer for SBR latex carpet backing, garment padding and shoe insoles.

Sodium Coconut N-Methyl Taurate

This is a chemically stable surfactant with good foaming, lathering and dispersing properties, used in shampoos, bubble baths and cosmetics.

Sodium Methyl Cocoyl Taurate

This is a primary or secondary anionic surfactant for shampoos and skin cleansers.

Sodium Tall Oil Acid N Methyl Taurate

This is used as a dispersing and suspending agent, which also has the ability to inhibit precipitation of salts such as barium, calcium and strontium. It also has the ability to prevent scale build up in oil well tubing and lines.

Sodium Cocoyl Isethionate

This is used in mild syndet/combo bar soaps, cosmetic preparations and even in stucco and spackling products.

Sodium Butoxy Ethyl Acetate

This is an extremely low foaming wetting agent, stabile in high acid and alkali mixtures. This is used in metal cleaning, bottle washing, steam cleaning, wax stripping and cleaning food prep areas.

CATIONIC SURFACTANTS

Cationic surfactants carry a positive charge on the hydrophilic portion of the surfactant. It is usually a nitrogen atom in the form of a quaternary ammonium compound, an amine salt or an imidazoline salt. Cationic surfactants are used in textile softeners, hair conditioners, germicides, antistats, corrosion inhibitors and specialty emulsifiers.

Cationics and Applications

Bezyl Trimonium Chloride
This is used as an effective corrosion inhibitor, used in germicidal cleaners and algaecides.

Cetylpyridinium Chloride
This is used in products as a corrosion inhibitor in oil well application.

Complex Ditallow Sulfate Quaternary
This is used in rinse cycle textile softeners for household and industrial laundry products. Also used as lubricants and softeners in textile application.

Cetyl Trimonium Bromide
This is an excellent conditioner for premium crème rinses and conditioners. It has superior antistatic, wet comb out and take up properties. It is effective on damaged hair and effective against gram positive and gram negative yeast organisms.

Cetyl Trimonium Chloride
This is used as a cationic hair conditioning agent with antistatic properties.

Myrtrimonium Bromide
This is used as an effective germicide used for disinfection of instrument, equipment, surfaces and skin products.

Lauramine Oxide
This surfactant is used to produce high flash foam in shampoos, bubble bath, dishwash, rug shampoos and fabric detergents.

Cocamine Oxide
This surfactant is used to produce high flash foam in shampoos, bubble bath, dishwash, rug shampoos and fabric detergents.

Coconut Hydroxyethyl Imidazoline

This is used to increase lubricity of water based cutting and grinding compounds. This is an effective antistat for wool and synthetic rugs and plastics. It is also a corrosion inhibitor.

Oleyl Hydroxyethyl Imidazoline

This is used for emulsifying carnuba wax and mineral oil for car wax emulsions. It is also a corrosion inhibitor for hydrochloric acid based solutions. It is also used as solvent emulsion cleaners. This surfactant has improved lubricity and anti corrosion properties in synthetic lubricates.

NONIONIC SURFACTANTS

Nonionic surfactants carry no charge, the hydrophilic portion usually contains numerous polar ether linkages derived from the polymerization of ethylene oxide and or propylene oxide with the hydrophobe. With nonionic surfactants as the number of moles of ethylene oxide increase on the hydrophobic base, the capacity for hydrogen bonding with water increases providing water solubility. Nonionic surfactants prove to be excellent emulsifiers, detergents, and wetting agents. They offer a wide range of capability as dispersants, solubilizers, coupling agents for cosmetics, textile applications, metal working, household, industrial and other diversified area.

Nonionics and applications

Alkanolamides
Alkanolamides are used in cosmetic and industrial applications, they provide performance and viscosity boosting for shampoos, skin cleaners, toiletries, detergents and dishwases. They are also useful as lubricants, anticorrosion agents dispersants, couplers, and emulsifiers.

Diethanolamide: Coconut (fatty acid)
This is useful as an economical foam booster and viscosity modifier; it is used in shampoos, bubble bath, liquid hand and body soaps, dishwashes, and household and industrial cleaners. These surfactants are also used in cosmetic applications and personal care products.

Diethanolamide: Coco/Lauric (fatty acid)
This is used as a foam stabilizer and thickening agent.

Diethanolamide: Lauric (fatty acid)
This is used as a foam booster and for stabilizing the foam. It can enhance viscosity and provides a increase in performance in hand and body soaps, shampoos, and related cosmetics.

Diethanolamide: Linoleic (fatty acid)
These are superfatting agent used for thickening for low active shampoos, bubble bath, and hand soaps. They also provide conditioning properties for hair and skin care products.

Mono-Ethanolamide: Coconut
These products add pearlescence, opacity, thickening, foam boosting, foam stabilization and mildness. These are used in detergents; toilet blocks as controlled release agents.

Mono-Isopropanolamide
These are used for powdered dishwash, bath and toiletry products. They also provide dry, brittle residue for carpet cleaners.

Alkanolamide: Coconut (fatty acid)
These are used in floor cleaner, all purpose cleaners, textile wet processing applications. They are also used as emulsifiers in solvent degreasers. These types of surfactants also provide rapid wetting, solubilizers and or emulsifiers for fats and grease. They also provide free rinsing, thickening and stable foam for pot and pan cleaners, dishwash liquids and carwash products.

Ethoxylated Alkanolamide: Coconut (fatty acid)
These are used for foam and thickening properties with improved alkali stability.

Nonionic Esters: Glycols
These products are used in cosmetics, hair care, skin care, and industrial products. They can function as emollients, emulsifiers, thickeners, pearlizers, dispersant, stabilizers and lubricates.

Diethylene Glycol Monostearate
These products are used for opacifiers, emollients and bodying agents for creams, lotions and shampoos.

Ethylene Glycol Distearate
These are used for opacifiers and pearlizing agents in personal care and detergents.

Ethylene Glycol Monostearate
These are used for pearlizing agents in shampoos, liquid hand and body soaps, and liquid detergents, also as emulsion stabilizers and thickeners.

Nonionic Esters: Glycerol
These products are used in cosmetics, hair care, skin care, and industrial products. They can function as emollients, emulsifiers, thickeners, pearlizers, dispersant, stabilizers and lubricates.

Glycerol Monostearate
These products are used as lipophilic emulsifiers for creams, lotions, sunscreens and antiperspirants, also as opacifiers and thickeners.

Nonionic Polyethylene Glycol Esters
These products have a wide range of applications. They can function as cosmetic emollients, industrial emulsifiers, textile processing, lubricants, defoamers, and as dispersants.

Polyethylene Glycol Dioleate

These can function as oil soluble emulsifiers for defoamers and fiber finishers; they add lubricity and are used in cosmetics as opacifiers. These products are also used as emulsifiers for oils, fats and solvents in metal working fluids, textile lubricants and in pesticides.

Polyethylene Glycol Oleate

These function as emulsifiers for fats and are useful in straight oils and soluble oils. They have a wide range of solubilities with good emulsification properties. They also provide lubricity and detergency. They can function as dye dispersants, textile finishing agents, emulsifiers in defoamers, cosmetics, and can be used as leveling agents in latex paints.

Nonionic Ethoxylated Oils

These products are used in cosmetics, hair care, skin care, and industrial products. They can function as emollients, emulsifiers, thickeners, pearlizers, dispersant, stabilizers and lubricates.

Ethoxylated Oils: Caster Oil

These are used as lubricants for synthetic fibers, leveling and dispersing agents for naphthol dyes, a co-emulsifier for herbicides, and metal working fluids. These surfactants can also be used for emulsifying fats, oils, fatty acids, waxes and solvents. They also function as coupling fluids, paper dye leveling agents and softening and rewetting agents for wetstrength paper. For paints the surfactant maintains the viscosity over a wide range of temperatures.

Nonionic Sorbitol and Ethoxylated Sorbitol Esters

These surfactants are found to be more effective emulsifiers for petroleum oils and waxes the polyethylene glycol ester surfactants. These surfactants have a wide range of emulsification properties for the lipophilic base. It has been found that these surfactants have good dispersant, antistat textile softening, lubrication, and stabilizing abilities.

Sorbitan Monolaurate

This is used as emulsifier/solubilizer for essential oils, fragrances and tars in cosmetics and pharmaceuticals. It is also used as thickeners in shampoos. These surfactants are also used as water dispersible emulsifiers for oils and fats in industrial products, coupler in mendicants, oils, fats and waxes in pharmaceuticals.

Sorbitan Trioleate

These are used in emulsifier/co-emulsifiers for oils, fats and waxes for textile, leather, fiberglass and metal lubricant products.

Nonionic Ethoxylates

This class of polyethers consists of nonylphenol ethoxylates and includes specialty surfactants used in cosmetic emollients, pesticide emulsifiers, and dispersants and for replacing chlorinated solvents in degreasing and other cleaning applications.

Octylphenol Aromatic Ethoxylates

These types of surfactants are used as effective emulsifiers for nonpolar solvents in solvent emulsion cleaners, cleaning detergents and floor polishes. These are also used as anti-icing additives in gasoline, solubilizer for hair colorants.

These surfactants are used in multiple types of detergents for textile, pulp and paper processing. These products are also used for controlled foam applications, emulsifier of solvents such as xylene. They also provide good hard surface detergency with high temperature stability, including stability in high acid and moderate alkalinity solutions. These surfactants provide good rinsability, avoid film formation and redeposition of soil in hot soak cleaner, and spray metal cleaners, electrolytic cleaning and acid pickling.

Nonylphenol Aromatic Ethoxylates

These surfactants have a broad range of applications such as: extremely oil soluble, stabilizes foam and have the ability to function as a defaomer in high concentration. They are used as soils soluble detergents and dispersion agents in petroleum oils. They are used as plasticizers and antistats for PVAc. They are also used as wetting agents, detergents in a wide range of applications, acid cleaners, and alkaline cleaners and as corrosion inhibitors.

Dinonylphenol Aromatic Ethoxylates

These surfactants are used in creating stable water in oil emulsions, soluble in polar and non polar solvents and ahs the ability to solubilize water into aliphatic solvents. These surfactants are used in acid cleaners, textile finishing oils, dry cleaning soaps, ink, lacquers, emulsions, metal working fluids, laundry compounds, floor cleaners, industrial cleaners, and synthetic detergents.

Dodecylphenol Aromatic Ethoxylates

These surfactants are used for all purpose emulsifiers and detergents in acid cleaners, sanitizers, grease cutting compounds, with low foaming and rewetting abilities.

Linear Alcohol Ethoxylates

These surfactants are biodegradable detergents, wetting agents and emulsifiers for household cleaners, laundry products, industrial metal cleaners, dairy cleaners, floor cleaners, wax strippers, and many other applications. They also are used as coupling agents in cosmetics and hair care products.

Oleyl Alcohol Ethoxylates

These are used as emulsifiers for mineral oils, fatty acids, waxes, liquid wax polishes, cosmetic creams, and lotions. They are acid stable for acid cleaning products and wetting agents.

Ethoxylated Mercaptans

These surfactants have exceptional wetting characteristics over wide water hardness, pH and temperature ranges. These are used in metal cleaning, oil and grease removal, all purpose hard surface cleaners, electronic cleaners, industrial laundry, and pre-spotting applications.

Block Polymers

These surfactants consist of two or more alkaline oxides attached to a low molecular weight organic compound. They are stable in acidic solutions and are soluble in aromatic solvents, chlorinated solvents, ethyl alcohol, and isopropyl alcohol. They are also soluble in butyl cellosolve, hexylene glycol and propylene glycol, but are not soluble in ethylene glycol, glycerin, kerosene and mineral oils. They are used in metal working bases, gelling agents, rinse aides, wetting agents, antistats, and defoamers.

General applications:

Rinse aide, automatic dishwashes, metal cleaners cutting fluids, hard surface cleaners, laundry cleaners, leveling agents, low to high foam applications, and industrial cleaners.

PHOSPHATE ESTERS

Phosphate ester surfactant can be either nonionic or anionic depending on the manufacturing process. Nonionic phosphate esters are complex phosphorylated nonionic surfactants which are stable and soluble in alkaline systems. Anionic phosphate esters are complex organic phosphates. These surfactants can be incorporated into dry cleaning solvents to assist in detergency, soil suspension and provide antistat properties.

Phosphate Ester: Aromatic
These are used for detergents, dry cleaning applications, corrosion inhibitors, and lubricity and anti friction applications.

Phosphate Ester: Aliphatic
These are used for emulsions, heat stability in acid cleaners, detergents, dry cleaning applications, corrosion inhibitors, and lubricity and anti friction applications.

Phosphate Ester: Alcohol Ethoxylate
This is used in soak tank cleaner applications, household and steam cleaner products.

Phosphate Ester: Linear Alcohol
This is used for gels, crud oils, and kerosene and diesel fuels.

Phosphate Ester: Nonylphenol Ethoxylate
This is a moderate foaming surfactant which is water and solvent soluble with good hard surface detergency. It has the ability to impart water rinsability to paint stripper, prolong floor finishers and antistat for carpet fibers.

Phosphate Ester: Polypropylene glycol Ethoxylate
This has low foam emulsifier characteristics with dispersant and rinsing properties. It is stable in high acid and alkali products.

Phosphate Ester: Linear Alcohol Ethoxylate
This has high monoester content with mild surfactant properties fir facial cleansers and in skin cleanser where dense foam is required.

Phosphate Ester: Linear Alcohol Alkoxylate
This surfactant is used for removing asphaltens, paraffins add scale materials. It is also recommended for difficult soils and alkaline spray and soak metal cleaner applications.

SPECIALTY SURFACTANTS

Specialty surfactants cover a broad range of materials. These proprietary surfactants are designed for specific performance and applications that the general amphoteric, cationic, anionic and nonionic surfactants can not provide. The areas in which these surfactants are used are:

Thickening
- Rice Starch
- Xanthan Gum
- Polysaccharides

Conditioning
- Polyquaternium-2
- Polyquaternium-7
- Poly Methacrylamidopropyl Trimonium Chloride

Dispersants
- Copolymer Sodium Salt
- Sodium Polyacrylate
- Sodium Polymethacrylate

Soil Repellents
- Proprietary components

Cleaner Concentrates
- Proprietary components

Pearlizing Agents
- Cold Blendable Pearl Concentrate

Skin Cleanser Concentrates
- Proprietary components
- Cetrimonium Bromide
- Stearalkonium Chloride

Personal Care Concentrates
- Disodium Cocoamphodiacetate
- Sodium Lauryl Sulfate
- Hexylene Glycol

Hand Soap Concentrate
- Disodium Lauroamphiacetate
- Sodium Trideceth Sulfate
- Hexylene Glycol
- PEG series

Antifoam/Defoamers
- Silicone base
- Nonsilicone-Oil Based

SILICONE SURFACTANTS

Silicone Fluids

Silicone fluids compromise a wide range of products which meet the demand for hundreds of application. The silicone fluids exhibit thermal and oxidation stability and are chemically inert with a wide range of materials such as: rubber, organic coatings, and fabricated materials. Most silicone fluids exhibit low viscosity, temperature coefficient ratios, stability to mechanical shear stress, and are non corrosive and non toxic. Because silicone fluids have a low surface tension they have the ability to spread easier and provide high surface activity to formulated products. Silicone fluids have hundreds of applications including defoamers, release agents, dampening, heat transfer and hydraulic fluids, textile finishes, and also in cosmetics for skin lotions and ointments.

Silicone Emulsions

Silicone emulsions are aqueous solutions of the silicone surfactant with water. They ate highly effective at low concentrations, chemically inert and generally do not discolor. Silicone emulsions are used as release aids in molding, extrusion, lamination and casting. Other application includes leather, glass vinyl cleaners, polishes, textile softeners; textile fiber lubricates foundry release agents, aerosol sprays and printing release agents.

CHELATING

In cleaning applications as well as other industrial processes metal ions can cause difficulties in the products performance. Metal ions can affect color, appearance, effectiveness and even the stability of a product. In order for a product or process to function effectively the metal ion are required to be removed which is quit difficult to accomplish. The solution to this problem is to inactivate the metal ions in solution; this is accomplished by chelating the metal ions.

Chelating agents securely bind the metal ions to form stable complexes which remain soluble in solution. The metal ions in this state are no longer have an affect in the product or processes.

There are a variety of chelating agents that can be used, so it is important for the formulator to select the appropriate chelating agent for the specific application to maximize the performance of the product.

The metal ion typically encounter are calcium, magnesium, iron, and copper. These metal ions may be "tied up" or inactivated in solution by adding the chelating agent which reacts to the corresponding metal ion, which creates the metal-chelate complex.

The reaction of the metal-chelate can be describe as follows; metal ions in solution normally exists with a positive charge (+). The chelator reacts strongly with the positive charge ions and converts them to a negative (-) charge metal-chelate compound.

In chelating it is important to know that the reaction moves in both directions, the reaction can be changed by adding or subtracting from either side. For example if we have a metal-chelate complex and acid is added to the solution, the pH is lowered causing the reaction to shift breaking the metal-chelate in to the metal ions and chelating agent. (Chelating works less in acid solutions)

GENERAL RULES ON CHELATION

Alkaline earth metal (calcium, magnesium, water hardness) are chelated in normal alkaline pH range usually held in solution and able to withstand the precipitation effects of most precipitating and scaling agents.

Magnesium ions will precipitate as the hydroxide in strong caustic solutions (5%) even in the presences of excess chelator.

Metal-chelates are stable down to approximately a pH of 2, except for the alkaline earth metals.

Chelating agents can prevent the precipitation of most common divalent metals by sulfide ion below the pH of 8.5.

Chelation-precipitation reactions are reversible and precipitates and scales will usually dissolve upon addition of a chelating agent are an adjustment of reaction conditions.

Chelator should always be used at the highest pH practical to the product or system.

Amphoteric metal, such as aluminum and chromium, are chelated in acidic or weakly alkaline solutions. As the pH increases to approximately 10 there is a gradual conversion to the aluminate and chromate anion with the release of the free chelating agent. [1, 6, 21, 23]

EXPERIMENT/TESTING METHOD

Design of experiments is one method used to achieve product performance and maintain quality and cost performance. Using DOE (Design of Experiments) in mixing experiments allows the formulator to gathering information on the performance of the individual ingredient and synergistic effects of the ingredients. DOE methodology includes the following:

1. **Comparison**: Comparing against a standard that acts as baseline.

2. **Randomization**: Variation of ingredient concentration with in the mixing samples. Random does not mean haphazard, and great care must be taken that appropriate methods are used.

3. **Replication**: Repeat measurements, so that the variability associated with the phenomenon can be estimated.

4. **Blocking**: Arrangement of experimental units into groups (blocks) that are similar to one another. Blocking reduces known but irrelevant sources of variation between units and thus allows greater precision in the estimation of the source of variation under study.

5. **Orthogonality**: Orthogonality concerns the forms of comparison (contrasts) that can be legitimately and efficiently carried out. Contrasts can be represented by vectors and sets of orthogonal contrasts are uncorrelated and independently distributed if the data are normal. Because of this independence, each orthogonal treatment provides different information to the others. If there are T treatments and T - 1 orthogonal contrast, all the information that can be captured from the experiment is obtainable from the set of contrasts.

6. **Use of factorial experiments instead of the one-factor-at-a-time method**. These are efficient at evaluating the effects and possible interactions of several factors (independent variables).

In evaluating a mixing/blending experiment it is important to identify and understand the following within the experiment:

Control variable: In the mixing experiment and data analysis, control variables are those variables that are not changed throughout the trials. The formulator is not interested in the effect of that particular variable being changed for that particular experiment. The control variables are extraneous factors, possibly affecting the experiment, that are kept constant so as to minimize their effects on the outcome. An example of a control variable in an experiment might be keeping the concentration of an alcohol at the same level throughout the experiment. In mixing experiments or tests, the controlled variable never changes; it is the same for every setup.

Independent variable: In mixing experiment or tests the independent variables, also called predictor variables, controlled variables, or manipulated variables, are those values that are controlled or selected by the formulator to determine its effect to an observed phenomenon (the dependent variable). In the mixing experiment the goal is to find evidence that the variation of the ingredients produces effects which provides data to determine the type of ingredient required and the concentration required.

Randomized test: Using randomized testing parameters reduces the formulator biases of the experiment. The mixing experiment is design so that the independent variable components (ingredients) are arranged in variable concentrations throughout the test. Typically three to four levels of variable concentrations are used in a random pattern or in a specific pattern which is design to show the interactions of the components.

Sample size: The sample size refers to the number of tests performed to validate the results of the experiment. A statistical sample is the number of repeated measurements that is typically denoted n, and is a non-negative integer.
Typically, different sample sizes lead to different accuracies of measurement. This can be seen in such statistical rules as the law of large numbers and the central limit theorem. Typically larger sample size n leads to increased precision in estimates of various properties within the experiment. Design of experiments methodologies have sample size included within the design structure.

Factorial experiment: Factorial experiment is an experiment whose design consists of two or more factors, each with discrete possible values or "levels", and whose experimental units take on all possible combinations of these levels across all such factors. Such an experiment allows studying the effect of each factor on the independent variables, as well as the effects of interactions between independent variables. For the vast majority of factorial experiments, each factor has only two levels. If the number of experiments for a full factorial design is too high, a fractional factorial design may be done, in which some of the possible combinations (usually at least half) are omitted.
The simplest factorial experiment contains two levels for each of two factors. Suppose a formulator needs to develop an ink remover, and has identified two chemicals that an effect on the ink. Component A works at 20% and component B works at 30%. The factorial experiment would

consist of four experimental units: component A at 20%, component B at 30%, component A at 20%, and component B at 20%, component A at 30%, component B at 30%, component A at 20%, and component B at 30%, component A at 30%, component B at 20%. Each combination of a single level selected from every factor is present once.

Two-level 2-Factor Full-Factorial Experiment Design Pattern

RUN	Combination	Factors	
		A	B
1	(1)	−	−
2	a	+	−
3	b	−	+
4 = 2^2	ab	+	+

For more than two factors, a 2k factorial experiment can be recursively designed from a 2k-1 factorial experiment by replicating the 2k-1 experiment, assigning the first replicate to the first (or low) level of the new factor, and the second replicate to the second (or high) level. This framework can be generalized to, e.g., designing three replicates for three level factors, etc.

Two-level 3-Factor Full-Factorial Experiment Design Pattern

RUN	Combination	Factors		
		A	B	C
1	(1)	−	−	−
2	a	+	−	−
3	b	−	+	−
4	ab	+	+	−
5	c	−	−	+
6	ac	+	−	+
7	bc	−	+	+
8 = 2^3	abc	+	+	+

Two-level 4-Factor Full-Factorial Experiment Design Pattern

RUN	Comb.	Factors			
		A	B	C	D
1	(1)	−	−	−	−
2	a	+	−	−	−
3	b	−	+	−	−
4	ab	+	+	−	−
5	c	−	−	+	−
6	ac	+	−	+	−
7	bc	−	+	+	−
8	abc	+	+	+	−

9	d	−	−	−	+
10	ad	+	−	−	+
11	bd	−	+	−	+
12	abd	+	+	−	+
13	cd	−	−	+	+
14	acd	+	−	+	+
15	bcd	−	+	+	+
16 = 2^4	abcd	+	+	+	+

A factorial experiment allows for estimation of experimental error in two ways. The experiment can be replicated, or the sparsity-of-effects principle can often be exploited. Replication is more common for small experiments and is a very reliable way of assessing experimental error. When the number of factors is large, typically greater than about 5 factors, replication of the design can become difficult. In these cases, it is common to only run a single replicate of the design, and to assume that factor interactions of more than three or more factors are negligible. Under this assumption, estimates of such high order interactions are estimates of an exact zero, thus really an estimate of experimental error.

When there are many factors, many experimental runs will be necessary, even without replication. For example, experimenting with 10 factors at two levels each produces 210=1024 combinations. At some point this becomes infeasible due to high cost or insufficient resources.

As with any statistical experiment, the experimental runs in a factorial experiment should be randomized to reduce the impact that bias could have on the experimental results. In practice, this can be a large operational challenge.

Factorial experiments can be used when there are more than two levels of each factor. However, the number of experimental runs required for three-level (or more) factorial designs will be considerably greater than for their two-level counterparts. Factorial designs are therefore less attractive if a researcher wishes to consider more than two levels. [24, 26]

ANALYSIS METHODS

Quality control through analysis is extremely important in product development and in production. Variations in the ratios of ingredients may cause problems in the performance of the product or increase the cost of the finished goods produced. Applying quality control methods reduces problems for the customer and maintains the product profit margins.

The following methods are used in analysis procedures to accomplish the quality standards required for the products developed, these are general methods.

Specific gravity

Specific gravity is utilized as a simple indicator for the mixture. Slight variations in the ratios can be seen using specific gravity of the solution (hydrometer method).

Specific gravity is the relative density or buoyancy of the solution. The rule of thumb for density is: if the solution is greater than 1, the object will be heavier than water and if it is less than 1, it will be lighter than water. It is important to measure the solution at a specific temperature for every measurement taken. [1, 23]

Hydrometer

A hydrometer is an instrument used for determining the specific gravity of liquids. It is usually made of glass and consists of a cylindrical stem and a bulb weighted with mercury or shot to make it float upright. The liquid is poured into a tall jar, and the hydrometer is gently lowered into the liquid until it floats freely.
The point where the surface of the liquid touches the stem of the hydrometer is noted. Hydrometers usually contain a paper scale inside the stem, so that the specific gravity (or density relative to water) can be read directly in grams per cubic centimeter.

In light liquids like kerosene, gasoline, and alcohol, the hydrometer must sink deeper to displace its weight of liquid than in heavy liquids like brine, milk, and acids. In fact, it is usual to have two separate instruments, one for heavy liquids, on which the mark 1.000 for water is near the top, and one for light liquids, on which the mark 1.000 is near the bottom of the stem. [1, 21, 23]

Viscosity

Viscosity is a measure of the resistance of a fluid to deform under shear stress. It is commonly perceived as "thickness" of the solution or resistance to flow. Viscosity is measured by laboratory viscometers such as the Brookfield viscometers.

Brookfield supplies the "Dial Viscometer". The viscosity is measured by spindles that are immersed in the solution at a specific temperature. The system measures the speed in which the spindle rotates to calculate the viscosity of the solution. [3, 4, 5]

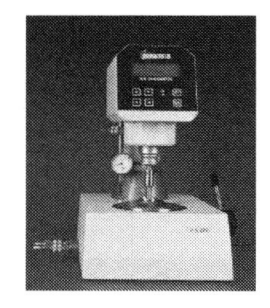

The following describes a few of their systems.

Dial Reading Viscometer - Available in 4 speed and 8 speed units. Readings are taken from the viscometer dial and converted into cP.

DV-E Viscometer
Available with 18 rotational speeds, 0.3 to 100 rpm. Displays cP or mPa, % Torque, Spindle and Speed.

pH-Meter

pH is a measure of the acidity or alkalinity of a solution. Solutions with a pH less than seven are considered acidic, while those with a pH greater than seven are considered basic (alkaline). pH 7 is considered neutral because it is the accepted pH of pure water at 25 °C, solution. Typically a pH meter is used to determine the pH of a solution.

A pH meter is an electronic instrument used to measure the pH (acidity or basicity) of a liquid (though special probes are sometimes used to measure the pH of semi-solid substances, such as cheese). A typical pH meter consists of a special measuring probe (a glass electrode) connected to an electronic meter that measures and displays the pH reading

The pH probe measures pH as the concentration of hydrogen ions surrounding a thin-walled glass bulb at its tip. The probe produces a small voltage (about 0.06 volt per pH unit) that is measured and displayed as pH units by the meter. For more information about pH probes, see glass electrode.

The meter circuit is fundamentally no more than a voltmeter that displays measurements in pH units instead of volts. The input impedance of the meter must be very high because of the high resistance — approximately 20 to 1000 MΩ (Megohms see ohm) — of the glass electrode probes typically used with pH meters. The circuit of a simple pH meter usually consists of operational amplifiers in an inverting configuration, with a total voltage gain of about -17. The inverting amplifier converts the small voltage produced by the probe (+0.059 volt/pH in basic solutions, -0.059 volt/pH in acid solutions) into pH units, which are then offset by 7 volts to give a reading on the pH scale. For example: At neutral pH (pH 7) the voltage at the probe's output is 0 volts. 0 * 17 + 7 = 7. At alkaline pH, the voltage at the probe's output ranges from > 0 to +0.41 volts (7 * 0.059 = 0.41). So for a sample of pH 10 (3 pH units from neutral), 3 * 0.059 = 0.18 volts), the output of the meter's amplifier is 0.18 * 17 + 7 = 10. At acid pH, the voltage at the probe's output ranges from -0.7 volts to < 0. So for a sample of pH 4 (also 3 pH units from neutral, but in the other direction), 3 * -0.059 = -0.18 volts, the output of the meter's amplifier is -0.18 * 17 + 7 = 4. [8]

pH meters range from simple and inexpensive pen-like devices to complex and expensive laboratory instruments with computer interfaces and several inputs for indicator (ion-sensitive, redox), reference electrodes, and temperature sensors such as thermoresistors or thermocouples. Cheaper models sometimes require that temperature measurements be entered to adjust for the slight variation in pH caused by temperature. Specialty meters and probes are available for use in special applications, harsh environments, etc. Pocket pH meter are readily available today for a few tens of dollars that automatically compensate for temperature. [8]

Conductivity

Conductivity is the ability of a material to conduct electric current. The principle by which instruments measure conductivity is simple — two plates are placed in the sample, a potential is applied across the plates (normally a sine wave voltage), and the current that passes through the solution is measured. Conductivity (G), the inverse of resistivity (R), is determined from the voltage and current values according to Ohm's law.

$$G = 1/R = I \text{ (amp)} / E \text{ (volts)}$$

Since the charge on ions in solution facilitates the conductance of electrical current, the conductivity of a solution is proportional to its ion concentration. In some situations, however, conductivity may not correlate

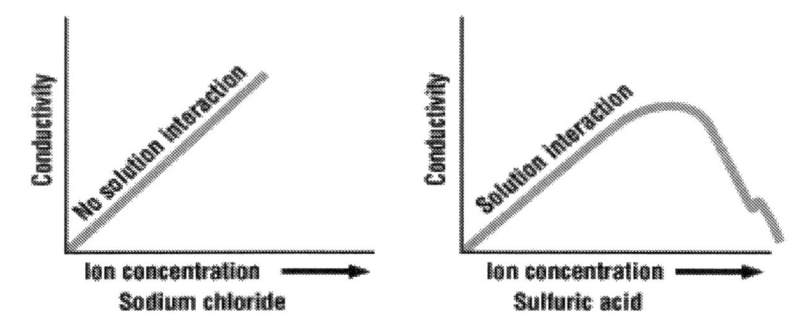

[Graphs: Conductivity vs. Ion concentration for Sodium chloride (linear, "No solution interaction") and Sulfuric acid ("Solution interaction", curve rises then falls)]

directly to concentration. The graph illustrates the relationship between conductivity and ion concentration for two common solutions. Notice that the graph is linear for sodium chloride solution, but not for highly concentrated sulfuric acid. Ionic interactions can alter the linear relationship between conductivity and concentration in some highly concentrated solutions.

The basic unit of conductance is the siemen (S), formerly called the mho. Since cell geometry affects conductivity values, standardized measurements are expressed in specific conductivity units (S/cm) to compensate for variations in electrode dimensions. Specific conductivity (C) is simply the product of measured conductivity (G) and the electrode cell constant (L/A), where L is the length of the column of liquid between the electrodes and A is the area of the electrodes (see illustration).
$C = G \times (L/A)$
If the cell constant (K) is 1 cm-1, the specific conductivity is the same as the measured conductivity of the solution. If other cell constants are used, most meters will automatically compensate for the change in cell geometry. To save room, cm-1 is not shown when cell constants are listed.
Although we specify conductivity ranges for our products in µS or mS, due to space limitations these ranges should be understood to reflect specific conductivity in µS/cm or mS/cm, respectively.

$$1 \text{ µS/cm} = 0.001 \text{ mS/cm} = 0.000001 \text{ S/cm} = 1 \text{ µmho/cm}$$

The following table shows optimum conductivity ranges for cells of three different constants:

Cell Constant(K)	Optimum Conductivity Range (µS/cm)
0.1	0.5 to 400
1.0	10 to 2000
10.0	1000 to 200,000

Conductivity meters and cells should be calibrated to a standard solution before using. Select a standard that is closest to the conductivity of the solution to be measured. Polarized or fouled electrodes must be replatinized or cleaned to renew active surface of the cell. In most situations, hot water with a mild liquid detergent is an effective cleanser. Acetone easily cleans most organic matter, and chlorous solutions will remove algae, bacteria, or molds. Do not use abrasives to clean an electrode. Replace this cell if all else fails.

Conductivity measurements are temperature dependent. The degree to which temperature affects conductivity varies from solution to solution and can be calculated using the following formula:

$$Gt = Gtcal\{1 + a(t-tcal)\}$$

where: Gt = conductivity at any temperature t in °C, $Gtcal$ = conductivity at calibration temperature $tcal$ in °C, a = temperature coefficient of solution at $tcal$ in °C,

Common alphas (a) are listed in the table below. To determine the a of other solutions, simply measure conductivity at a range of temperatures and graph the change in conductivity versus the change in temperature. Divide the slope of the graph by $Gtcal$ to get a.

Substance at 25°C	Concentration	Alpha (a)
HCl	10 wt%	1.56
KCl	10 wt%	1.88
H2SO4	50 wt%	1.93
NaCl	10 wt%	2.14
HF	1.5 wt%	7.20
HNO3	31 wt%	31.0

Most conductivity meters have a two-electrode cell available in either dip or flow-through styles. The electrode surface is usually platinum, titanium, gold-plated nickel, or graphite.

Four-electrode cells use a reference voltage to compensate for any polarization or fouling of the electrode plates. The reference voltage ensures that measurements indicate actual conductivity independent of electrode condition, resulting in higher accuracy for measuring over wide ranges. [1, 8, 21, 23]

Important Features to Consider

Autoranging: Meter automatically selects the appropriate range for measurement. There is no need to change the dial, multiply values on the display, turn a potentiometer, or manually select a range.

Temperature compensation: A cell with built-in temperature sensor allows the meter to make adjustments to the conductivity or TDS readings based on changes in solution temperature.

TDS conversion factor: When a solution does not have a similar ionic content to natural water or salt water, then a TDS conversion factor is needed to automatically adjust the readings.

Adjustable temperature coefficients: The TDS of certain samples, such as alcohols and pure water, are affected by changes in temperature. An adjustable temperature coefficient allows the user to compensate for temperature changes on the solution being measured.

Adjustable cell constant: Adjusts the reading on the display to reflect use of a cell with a constant other than K=1.

Titration

Titration is a common laboratory method of quantitative/chemical analysis which can be used to determine the concentration of a known reactant. Because volume measurements play a key role in titration, it is also known as volumetric analysis. A reagent, called the titrant, of known concentration (a standard solution) and volume is used to react with a measured quantity of reactant (the analyte). Using a calibrated burette to add the titrant, it is possible to determine the exact amount that has been consumed when the endpoint is reached. The endpoint is the point at which the titration is stopped. This is classically a point at which the number of moles of titrant is equal to the number of moles of analyte, or some multiple thereof (as in polyprotic acids).

In the classic strong acid-strong base titration the endpoint of a titration is when the pH of the reactant is just about equal to 7, and often when the solution permanently changes color due to an indicator. There are however many different types of titrations.

Many methods can be used to indicate the endpoint of a reaction; titrations often use visual indicators (the reactant mixture changes color). In simple acid-base titrations a pH indicator may be used, such as phenolphthalein, which becomes pink when a certain pH (about 8.2) is reached or exceeded. Another example is methyl orange, which is red in acids and yellow in alkali solutions.

Not every titration requires an indicator. In some cases, either the reactants or the products are strongly colored and can serve as the "indicator". For example, an oxidation-reduction titration using potassium permanganate (pink/purple) as the titrant does not require an indicator. When the titrant is reduced, it turns colorless. After the equivalence point, there is excess titrant present. The equivalence point is identified from the first faint pink color that persists in the solution being titrated.

Due to the logarithmic nature of the pH curve, the transitions are generally extremely sharp, and thus a single drop of titrant just before the endpoint can change the pH significantly leading to an immediate color change in the indicator. There is a slight difference between the change in indicator color and the actual equivalence point of the titration. This error is referred to as an indicator error, and it is indeterminate.

A typical titration begins with a beaker or Erlenmeyer flask containing a precisely known volume of the reactant and a small amount of indicator, placed underneath a burette containing the reagent. By controlling the amount of reagent that is added to the reactant, it is possible to detect the point at which the indicator changes color. As long as the indicator has been chosen correctly, this should also be the point where the reactant and reagent neutralize each other, and by reading the scale on the burette the volume of reagent can be measured.

As the concentration of the reagent is known, the number of moles of reagent can be calculated (since concentration = moles / volume). Then, from the chemical equation involving the two substances, the number of moles present in the reactant can be found. Finally, by dividing the number of moles of reactant by its volume, the concentration is calculated.

Titrations are often recorded on titration curves, whose compositions are generally identical: the independent variable is the volume of the titrant, while the dependent variable is the pH of the solution (which changes depending on the composition of the two solutions). The equivalence point is a significant point on the graph (the point at which all of the starting solution, usually an acid, has been neutralized by the titrant, usually a base). It can be calculated precisely by finding the second derivative of the titration curve and computing the points of inflection (where the graph changes concavity); however, in most cases, simple visual inspection of the curve will suffice (in the curve given to the right, both equivalence points are visible, after roughly 15 and 30 mL of NaOH solution has been titrated into the oxalic acid solution.) To calculate the pKa values, one must find the volume at the half-equivalence point, which is where half the amount of titrant has been added to form the next compound (here, sodium hydrogen oxalate, and then disodium oxalate). Halfway between each equivalence point, at 7.5 mL and 22.5 mL, the pH observed was about 1.5 and 4, giving the pKa values.

In monoprotic acids, the point halfway between the beginning of the curve (before any titrant has been added) and the equivalence point is significant: at that point, the concentrations of the two solutions (the titrant and the original solution) are equal. Therefore, the Henderson-Hasselbalch equation can be solved in this manner: [1, 21, 23]

$$pH = pK_a + log\frac{([base])}{([acid])}$$

$$pH = pK_a + log(1)$$

$$pH = pK_a$$

Therefore, one can easily find the acid dissociation constant of the monoprotic acid by finding the pH of the point halfway between the beginning of the curve and the equivalence point, and solving the simplified equation. In the case of the sample curve, the Ka would be approximately 1.78×10-5 from visual inspection (the actual Ka2 is 1.7×10-5). For polyprotic acids, calculating the acid dissociation constants is only marginally more difficult: the first acid dissociation constant can be calculated the same way as it would be calculated in a monoprotic acid. The second acid dissociation constant, however, is the point halfway between the first equivalence point and the second equivalence point (and so on for acids that release more than two protons, such as phosphoric acid).

Titrations can be classified by the type of reaction. Different types of titration reaction include:

Acid-base titration is based on the neutralization reaction between the analyte and an acidic or basic titrant. These most commonly use a pH indicator, a pH meter, or a conductance meter to determine the endpoint.

A **Redox titration** is based on an oxidation-reduction reaction between the analyte and titrant. These most commonly use a potentiometer or a redox indicator to determine the endpoint. Frequently either the reactants or the titrant have a color intense enough that an additional indicator is not needed.

A **Complex metric titration** is based on the formation of a complex between the analyte and the titrant. The chelating agent EDTA is very commonly used to titrate metal ions in solution. These titrations generally require specialized indicators that form weaker complexes with the analyte. A common example is Eriochrome Black T for the titration of calcium and magnesium ions. [1, 2, 6, 7, 21, 23]

Qualitative Analysis

Identifying Anions and Cations

Qualitative analysis can be used to separate and detect cations and anions in quality control production analysis.

First, ions are removed in groups from the initial aqueous solution. After each group has been separated, then testing is conducted for the individual ions in each group. Here is a common grouping of cations:

Group I: Ag^+, Hg_2^{2+}, Pb^{2+}
Precipitated in 1 M HCl

Group II: Bi^{3+}, Cd^{2+}, Cu^{2+}, Hg^{2+}, (Pb^{2+}), Sb^{3+} and Sb^{5+}, Sn^{2+} and Sn^{4+}
Precipitated in 0.1 M H_2S solution at pH 0.5

Group III: Al^{3+}, (Cd^{2+}), Co^{2+}, Cr^{3+}, Fe^{2+} and Fe^{3+}, Mn^{2+}, Ni^{2+}, Zn^{2+}
Precipitated in 0.1 M H_2S solution at pH 9

Group IV: Ba^{2+}, Ca^{2+}, K^+, Mg^{2+}, Na^+, NH_4^+
Ba^{2+}, Ca^{2+}, and Mg^{2+} are precipitated in 0.2 M $(NH_4)_2CO_3$ solution at pH 10; the other ions are soluble

Many reagents are used in qualitative analysis, but only a few are involved in nearly every group procedure. The four most commonly used reagents are 6M HCl, 6M HNO_3, 6M NaOH, 6M NH_3. Understanding the uses of the reagents is helpful when planning an analysis.

Among the most common reactions in qualitative analysis are those involving the formation or decomposition of complex ions and precipitation reactions. These reactions may be performed directly by adding the appropriate anion, or a reagent such as H2S or NH3 may dissociate in water to furnish the anion. Strong acid may be used to dissolve precipitates containing a basic anion. Ammonia or sodium hydroxide may be used to bring a solid into solution if the cation in the precipitate forms a stable complex with NH3 or OH-.

A cation is usually present as a single principal species, which may be a complex ion, free ion, or precipitate. If the reaction goes to completion the principal species is a complex ion. The precipitate is the principal species if most of the precipitate remains undissolved.

If a cation forms a stable complex the addition of a complexing agent at 1 M or greater generally will convert the free ion to complex ion.
The dissociation constant Kd can be used to determine the extent to which a cation is converted to a complex ion. The solubility product constant Ksp can be used to determine the fraction of cation remaining in a solution after precipitation. Kd and Ksp are both required to calculate the equilibrium constant for dissolving a precipitate in a complexing agent. [1, 2, 6, 7, 21, 23]

ADDITIONAL ANALYSIS EQUIPMENT

Atomic absorption spectroscopy

Atomic absorption spectroscopy in analytical chemistry is a technique for determining the concentration of a particular metal element within a sample. Atomic absorption spectroscopy can be used to analyze the concentration of over 62 different metals in a solution.

The technique makes use of a flame to atomize the sample, but other atomizers such as a graphite furnace are also used. Three steps are involved in turning a liquid sample into an atomic gas:

Desolvation – the liquid solvent is evaporated, and the dry sample remains

Vaporization – the solid sample vaporizes to a gas

Volatilization – the compounds making up the sample are broken into free atoms.

The flame is arranged such that it is laterally long (usually 10cm) and not deep. The height of the flame must also be controlled by controlling the flow of the fuel mixture. A beam of light is focused through this flame at its longest axis (the lateral axis) onto a detector past the flame.
The light that is focused into the flame is produced by a hollow cathode lamp. Inside the lamp is a cylindrical metal cathode containing the metal for excitation, and an anode.

When a high voltage is applied across the anode and cathode, the metal atoms in the cathode are excited into producing light with a certain emission spectra. The type of hollow cathode tube depends on the metal being analyzed. For analyzing the concentration of copper in an ore, a copper cathode tube would be used, and likewise for any other metal being analyzed. The electrons of the atoms in the flame can be promoted to higher orbitals for an instant by absorbing a set quantity of energy (a quantum). This amount of energy is specific to a particular electron transition in a particular element. As the quantity of energy put into the flame is known, and the quantity remaining at the other side (at the detector) can be measured, it is possible to calculate how many of these transitions took place, and thus get a signal that is proportional to the concentration of the element being measured. [23]

GC/MS

Gas chromatography-mass spectrometry (GC-MS) is a method that combines the features of gas-liquid chromatography and mass spectrometry to identify different substances within a test sample. Applications of GC-MS include drug detection, fire investigation, environmental analysis, and explosives investigation. GC-MS can also be used in airport security to detect substances in luggage or on human beings. Additionally, it can identify trace elements in materials that were previously thought to have disintegrated beyond identification.
The GC-MS has been widely heralded as a "gold standard" for forensic substance identification because it is used to perform a specific test. A specific test positively identifies the actual presence of a particular substance in a given sample. A non-specific test, however, merely indicates that a substance falls into a category of substances. Although a non-specific test could statistically suggest the identity of the substance, this could lead to false positive identification.

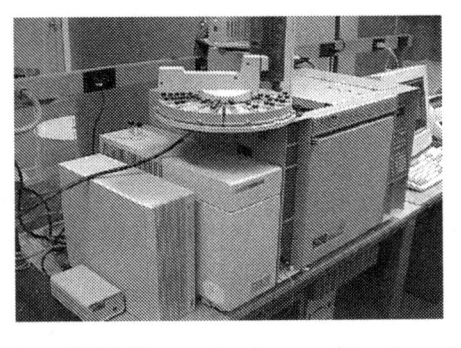

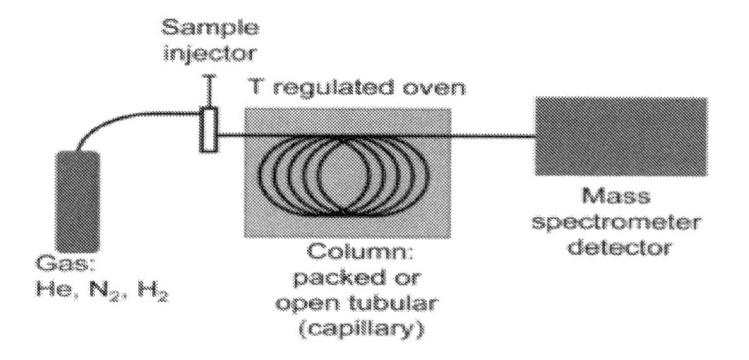

GC-MS schematic

The GC-MS is composed of two major building blocks: the gas chromatograph and the mass spectrometer. The gas chromatograph uses the difference in the chemical properties between different molecules in a mixture to separate the molecules. The molecules take different amounts of time (called the retention time) to come out of the gas chromatograph, and this allows the mass spectrometer downstream to evaluate the molecules separately in order to identify them. The mass spectrometer does this by breaking each molecule into ionized fragments and detecting these fragments using their mass to charge ratio. Each molecule has a specific fragment spectrum which allows for its detection.

These two components, used together, allow a much finer degree of substance identification than either unit used separately. It is possible to make an accurate identification of a particular molecule by gas chromatography or mass spectrometry alone. The mass spectrometry process normally requires a very pure sample while gas chromatography can be confused by different molecular types that both happen to take about the same amount of time to travel through the unit (i.e. have the same retention time). Sometimes two different molecules can also have a similar pattern of ionized fragments in a mass spectrometer (mass spectrum). Combining the two processes makes it extremely unlikely that two different molecules will behave in the same way in both a gas chromatograph and a mass spectrometer. So when an identifying mass spectrum appears at a characteristic retention time in a GC-MS analysis, it is usually taken as proof of the presence of that particular molecule in the sample. [17]

Ion-exchange chromatography

Ion-exchange chromatography (or ion chromatography) is a process that allows the separation of ions and polar molecules based on the charge properties of the molecules. It can be used for almost any kind of charged molecule including large proteins, small nucleotides and amino acids, with the experimental solution to be separated collectively known as the analyte. It is often used as a first step in protein purification.

Ion exchange chromatography retains analyte molecules based on coulombic (ionic) interactions. The stationary phase surface displays ionic functional groups that interact with analyte ions of opposite charge. This type of chromatography is further subdivided into cation exchange chromatography and anion exchange chromatography:

Cation exchange chromatography retains positively charged cations because the stationary phase displays a negatively charged functional group such as a phosphoric acid.

Anion exchange chromatography retains negatively charged anions using positively charged functional group such as a quaternary ammonium cation.

Typical Technique: A sample is introduced, either manually or with an autosampler, into a sample loop of known volume. A buffered aqueous solution known as the mobile phase carries the sample from the loop onto a column that contains some form of stationary phase material. This is typically a resin or gel matrix consisting of agarose or cellulose beads with covalently bonded charged functional groups. The target analytes (anions or cations) are retained on the stationary phase but can be eluted by increasing the concentration of a similarly charged species that will displace the analyte ions from the stationary phase. For example, in cation exchange chromatography, the positively charged analyte could be displaced by the addition of positively charged sodium ions. The analytes of interest must then be detected by some means, typically by conductivity or UV/Visible light absorbance.
In order to control an IC system, a Chromatography Data System (CDS) is usually needed. In addition to IC systems, some of these CDSs can also control Gas Chromatography (GC) and HPLC systems. [1, 17, 21, 23]

FTIR Spectroscopy

FTIR (Fourier Transform Infrared) Spectroscopy, or simply FTIR Analysis, is an analysis technique that provides information about the chemical bonding or molecular structure of materials, whether organic or inorganic. It is used in analysis to identify unknown materials present in a specimen.

The technique works on the fact that bonds and groups of bonds vibrate at characteristic frequencies. A molecule that is exposed to infrared rays absorbs infrared energy at frequencies which are characteristic to that molecule. During FTIR analysis, a spot on the specimen is subjected to a modulated IR beam. The specimen's transmittance and reflectance of the infrared rays at different frequencies is translated into an IR absorption plot consisting of reverse peaks. The resulting FTIR spectral pattern is then analyzed and matched with known signatures of identified materials in the FTIR library.

FTIR spectroscopy does not require a vacuum, since neither oxygen nor nitrogen absorb infrared rays. FTIR analysis can be applied to minute quantities of materials, whether solid, liquid, or gaseous. When the library of FTIR spectral patterns does not provide an acceptable match, individual peaks in the FTIR plot may be used to yield partial information about the specimen.

Single fibers or particles are sufficient enough for material identification through FTIR analysis. Organic contaminants in solvents may also be analyzed by first separating the mixture into its components by gas chromatography, and then analyzing each component by FTIR. [17]

Ultraviolet-visible spectroscopy or ultraviolet-visible spectrophotometer (UV/ VIS)

Ultraviolet-visible spectroscopy or ultraviolet-visible spectrophotometer (UV/ VIS) involves the spectroscopy of photons and spectrophotometer. It uses light in the visible and adjacent near ultraviolet (UV) and near infrared (NIR) ranges. In this region of energy space molecules undergo electronic transitions.

UV/VIS spectroscopy is routinely used in the quantitative determination of solutions of transition metal ions and highly conjugated organic compounds.
Solutions of transition metal ions can be colored (i.e., absorb visible light) because d electrons within the metal atoms can be excited from one electronic state to another. The color of metal ion solutions is strongly affected by the presence of other species, such as certain anions or ligands. For instance, the color of a dilute solution of copper sulphate is a very light blue; adding ammonia intensifies the color and changes the wavelength of maximum absorption (λ_max).

Organic compounds, especially those with a high degree of conjugation, also absorb light in the UV or visible regions of the electromagnetic spectrum. The solvents for these determinations are often water for water soluble compounds, or ethanol for organic-soluble compounds. (Organic solvents may have significant UV absorption; not all solvents are suitable for use in UV spectroscopy. Ethanol absorbs very weakly at most wavelengths.)
While charge transfer complexes also give rise to colors, the colors are often too intense to be used for quantitative measurement.

The Beer-Lambert law states that the absorbance of a solution is directly proportional to the solution's concentration. Thus UV/VIS spectroscopy can be used to determine the concentration of a solution. It is necessary to know how quickly the absorbance changes with concentration. This can be taken from references (tables of molar extinction coefficients), or more accurately, determined from a calibration curve.

A UV/VIS spectrophotometer may be used as a detector for HPLC. The presence of an analyte gives a response which can be assumed to be proportional to the concentration. For accurate results, the instrument's response to the analyte in the unknown should be compared with the response to a standard; this is very similar to the use of calibration curves. The response (e.g., peak height) for a particular concentration is known as the response factor. [17]

High-performance liquid chromatography (HPLC)

High-performance liquid chromatography (HPLC) is a form of column chromatography used frequently in biochemistry and analytical chemistry. It is also sometimes referred to as high-pressure liquid chromatography. HPLC is used to separate components of a mixture by using a variety of chemical interactions between the substance being analyzed (analyte) and the chromatography column.

In isocratic HPLC the analyte is forced through a column of the stationary phase (usually a tube packed with small round particles with a certain surface chemistry) by pumping a liquid (mobile phase) at high pressure through the column. The sample to be analyzed is introduced in a small volume to the stream of mobile phase and is retarded by specific chemical or physical interactions with the stationary phase as it traverses the length of the column. The amount of retardation depends on the nature of the analyte, stationary phase and mobile phase composition. The time at which a specific analyte elutes (comes out of the end of the column) is called the retention time and is considered a reasonably unique identifying characteristic of a given analyte. The use of pressure increases the linear velocity (speed) giving the components less time to diffuse within the column, leading to improved resolution in the resulting chromatogram.

Common solvents used include any miscible combinations of water or various organic liquids (the most common are methanol and acetonitrile). Water may contain buffers or salts to assist in the separation of the analyte components, or compounds such as Trifluoroacetic acid which acts as an ion pairing agent.

A further refinement to HPLC has been to vary the mobile phase composition during the analysis; this is known as gradient elution. A normal gradient for reverse phase chromatography might start at 5% methanol and progress linearly to 50% methanol over 25 minutes, depending on how hydrophobic the analyte is. The gradient separates the analyte mixtures as a function of the affinity of the analyte for the current mobile phase composition relative to the stationary phase. This partitioning process is similar to that which occurs during a liquid-liquid extraction but is continuous, not step-wise. In this example, using a water/methanol gradient, the more hydrophobic components will elute (come off the column) under conditions of relatively high methanol; whereas the more hydrophilic compounds will elute under conditions of relatively low methanol. The choice of solvents, additives and gradient depend on the nature of the stationary phase and the analyte. Often a series of tests are performed on the analyte and a number of generic runs may be processed in order to find the optimum HPLC method for the analyte - the method which gives the best separation of peaks.

Normal phase chromatography

Normal phase HPLC (NP-HPLC) was the first kind of HPLC chemistry used, and separates analytes based on polarity. This method uses a polar stationary phase and a nonpolar mobile phase, and is used when the analyte of interest is fairly polar in nature. The polar analyte associates with and is retained by the polar stationary phase. Adsorption strengths increase with increase in analyte polarity, and the interaction between the polar analyte and the polar stationary phase (relative to the mobile phase) increases the elution time. The interaction strength not only depends on the functional groups in the analyte molecule, but also on steric factors and structural isomers are often resolved from one another. Use of more polar solvents in the mobile phase will decrease the retention time of the analytes while more hydrophobic solvents tend to increase retention times. Particularly polar solvents in a mixture tend to deactivate the column by occupying the stationary phase surface. This is somewhat particular to normal phase because it is most purely an adsorptive mechanism (the interactions are with a hard surface rather than a soft layer on a surface). NP-HPLC had fallen out of favor in the 1970's with the development of reversed-phase HPLC because of a lack of reproducibility of retention times as water or protic organic solvents changed the hydration state of the silica or alumina chromatographic media. Recently it has become useful again with the development of HILIC bonded phases which utilize a partition mechanism which provides reproducibility.

Reversed phase chromatography

Reversed phase HPLC (RP-HPLC) consists of a non-polar stationary phase and a moderately polar mobile phase. One common stationary phase is a silica which has been treated with RMe_2SiCl, where R is a straight chain alkyl group such as $C_{18}H_{37}$ or C_8H_{17}. The retention time is therefore longer for molecules which are more non-polar in nature, allowing polar molecules to elute more readily. Retention time is increased by the addition of polar solvent to the mobile phase and decreased by the addition of more hydrophobic solvent. Reversed phase chromatography is so commonly used that it is not uncommon for it to be incorrectly referred to as "HPLC" without further specification.

RP-HPLC operates on the principle of hydrophobic interactions which result from repulsive forces between a relatively polar solvent, the relatively non-polar analyte, and the non-polar stationary phase. The driving force in the binding of the analyte to the stationary phase is the decrease in the area of the non-polar segment of the analyte molecule exposed to the solvent. This hydrophobic effect is dominated by the decrease in free energy from entropy associated with the minimization of the ordered molecule-polar solvent interface. The hydrophobic effect is decreased by adding more non-polar solvent into the mobile phase. This shifts the partition coefficient such that the analyte spends some portion of time moving down the column in the mobile phase, eventually eluting from the column.

The characteristics of the analyte molecule play an important role in its retention characteristics. In general, an analyte with a longer alkyl chain length results in a longer retention time because it increases the molecule's hydrophobicity. Very large molecules, however, can result in incomplete interaction between the large analyte surface and the alkyl chain. Retention time increases with hydrophobic surface area which is roughly inversely proportional to solute size. Branched chain compounds elute more rapidly than their corresponding isomers because the overall surface area is decreased.

Aside from mobile phase hydrophobicity, other mobile phase modifiers can affect analyte retention. For example, the addition of inorganic salts causes a linear increase in the surface tension of aqueous solutions, and because the entropy of the analyte-solvent interface is controlled by surface tension, the additions of salts tend to increase the retention time. Another important component is pH since this can change the hydrophobicity of the analyte. For this reason most methods use a buffering agent, such as sodium phosphate to control the pH. An organic acid such as formic acid or most commonly trifluoroacetic acid is often added to the mobile phase. These serve multiple purposes: They control pH, neutralize the charge on any residual exposed silica on the stationary phase and act as ion pairing agents to neutralize charge on the analyte. The effect varies depending on use but generally improve the chromatography.

Reversed phase columns are quite difficult to damage compared with normal silica columns, however, many reverse phase columns consist of alkyl derivatized silica particles and should never be used with aqueous bases as these will destroy the underlying silica backbone. They can be used with aqueous acid but the column should not be exposed to the acid for too long, as it can corrode the metal parts of the HPLC equipment. The metal content of HPLC columns must be kept low if the best possible ability to separate substances is to be retained. A good test for the metal content of a column is to inject a sample which is a mixture of 2,2'- and 4,4'-bipyridine. Because the 2,2'-bipy can chelate the metal it is normal that when a metal ion is present on the surface of the silica the shape of the peak for the 2,2'-bipy will be distorted, tailing will be seen on this distorted peak.

Size exclusion chromatography

Size exclusion chromatography (SEC), also known as gel permeation chromatography or gel filtration chromatography, separates particles on the basis of size. It is generally a low resolution chromatography and thus it is often reserved for the final, "polishing" step of purification. It is also useful for determining the tertiary structure and quaternary structure of purified proteins, and is the primary technique for determining the average molecular weight of natural and synthetic polymers.

Ion exchange chromatography

In Ion-exchange chromatography, retention is based on the attraction between solute ions and charged sites bound to the stationary phase. Ions of the same charge are excluded. Some types of Ion Exchangers include: (1) Polystyrene resins- allows cross linkage which increases the stability of the chain. Higher cross linkage reduces swerving, which increases the equilibration time and ultimately improves selectivity. (2) Cellulose and dextrin ion exchangers (gels)-These possess larger pore sizes and low charge densities making them suitable for protein separation. (3)Controlled-pore glass or porous silica. In general, ion exchangers favor the binding of ions of higher charge and smaller radius.
An increase in counter ion (with respect to the functional groups in resins) concentration reduces the retention time. An increase in pH reduces the retention time in cation exchange while a decrease in pH reduces the retention time in anion exchange.
This form of chromatography is widely used in the following applications: In purifying water, preconcentration of trace components, Ligand-exchange chromatography, Ion-exchange chromatography of proteins, High-pH anion-exchange chromatography of carbohydrates and oligosaccharides, etc.

Bioaffinity chromatography

This chromatographic process relies on the property of biologically active substances to form stable, specific, and reversible complexes. The formation of these complexes involves the participation of common molecular forces such as the Van der Waal's interaction, electrostatic interaction, dipole-dipole interaction, hydrophobic interaction, and the hydrogen bond. An efficient, biospecific bond is formed by a simultaneous and concerted action of several of these forces in the complementary binding sites. [16, 17, 18]

CHEMICAL MIXING/BLENDING

Mixing/blending of chemical components is an important aspect of formulating in liquid-liquid components. Even thought it might seem simple, just mixing the ingredients together in a container, there are a number of factors the formulator must consider before blending the components.

Units of measure

The two units of measure are volume and weight for liquid-liquid components. Weight is the most commonly used, due to the fact that certain chemical volumes fluctuate through temperature. Small volume mixes will usually have a slight variation in volume/volume mixes. In large scale production applications this variation in liquid-liquid components can have a dramatic effect on the final volume of the product manufactured. Using weight measurement application minimizes the variation see in volume measurements.

Chemical Compatibility

There are a number of materials that mixing tanks can be constructed from, such as polypropylene, polyethylene, fiberglass, carbon steel stainless steel and others. The characteristics of the product will determine the type of mixing vessel required. It is important to identify the chemical compatibility of each type of tank with the chemical components in the product.

Chemical Compatibility Chart

Legend:
- ● Good
- ◐ Fair
- ◑ Poor
- ✕ Don't Use
- — No Data

	Metals				Plastics							Seals				
	316 Stainless	Aluminum	Brass	Carbon Steel	Kynar	PVC	Teflon	ABS	Polyethylene	Polypropylene	Ryton	Viton	Nitrile/Buna N	Neoprene	Ethylene Propylene	Ceramic
Acetic Acid	Good	Fair	Poor	Poor	Good	Good	Good	Poor	Good	Good	Good	Poor	Fair	Fair	Good	Good
Acetone	Good	Good	Good	Good	Don't Use	Don't Use	Good	No Data	Fair	Fair	Good	Don't Use	Don't Use	Fair	Good	Good

Chemical															
Acetylene[2]	●	●	-	●	-	◐	-	✕	-	✕	●	●	●	◐	●	●
Acidic Mine Water	●	◐	✕	-	-	●	-	◐	-	●	◐	●	●	●	-	●
Acrylonitrile	◐	◐	-	-	-	-	-	-	-	●	●	✕	✕	◐	●	●
Ammonium Chloride	◐	◐	◐	✕	●	●	●	-	◐	●	●	●	●	●	●	●
Ammonium Hydroxide	●	◐	✕	◐	-	●	●	◐	●	●	●	◐	◐	●	●	●
Ammonium Sulfate	◐	◐	◐	◐	●	●	●	-	◐	●	●	●	✕	●	●	●
Ammonium Thio-Sulfate	●	-	-	●	-	-	-	-	-	-	-	-	-	●	-	●
Anhydrous Ammonia	●	◐	-	◐	✕	●	●	-	●	●	◐	✕	◐	●	●	●
Calcium Carbonate	●	✕	-	-	-	●	●	-	●	-	-	●	-	●	-	●
Calcium Chloride	✕	✕	-	-	●	●	●	◐	◐	●	●	●	✕	●	●	●
Calcium Hydroxide	●	✕	-	-	-	●	●	-	◐	●	-	●	●	●	●	●
Calcium Hypochlorite	◐	✕	-	-	●	✕	●	-	◐	●	-	●	◐	✕	●	●
Calcium Sulfate	●	◐	-	-	●	●	●	◐	●	●	●	●	✕	-	●	●
Carbon Monoxide	●	●	-	-	-	●	●	-	◐	●	●	●	●	◐	●	●
Carbon Tetrachloride[1,2]	◐	◐	●	✕	●	◐	✕	✕	✕	◐	●	●	◐	✕	-	●
Carbonated Water	●	●	-	-	-	●	-	-	-	●	-	●	●	●	●	●
Carbonic Acid	◐	●	-	-	●	●	●	-	◐	●	-	●	◐	●	●	●
Chlorine	●	✕	◐	-	-	-	●	-	-	-	●	◐	✕	-	✕	●
Chlorine Water	✕	✕	✕	-	●	●	●	-	-	✕	◐	●	✕	◐	✕	●
Chromic Acid 50%[5]	◐	◐	✕	-	◐	◐	◐	◐	◐	◐	●	✕	✕	●	●	●
Citric Acid	●	◐	◐	-	●	●	●	◐	◐	-	●	✕	●	●	●	●

Order of Addition

In developing a product it is important to determine the order of addition of the chemical components of the product, especially in emulsions and coupled products.

Emulsions: oil in water (o/w) and water in oil (w/o) require specific order of addition with the emulsifying agent. If the order is out of sequence the emulsion will not form. Oil/water form or water/oil form depends not only on the emulsifier selected but the mixing speed and temperature as well. The ratio between components is also a factor in creating a stable emulsion. Depending on the stability required an emulsion can be considered usable from minutes to years depending on the intended use. Shelf life testing is very important aspect in development of emulsion products.

In products that contain acid or alkali materials, it is extremely important that the acid is added to the water a slow rate, heat will be generated, and similarly the alkali must be added to the water at a slow rate as well. Heat will be generated with this material as well.

Physical Mixing

Design of equipment for mixing depends on the physical properties of the individual components and that of the final admixture, the degree of homogeneity desired, and the time scale of the mixing process. For example, equipment designed to mix high viscosity, non-Newtonian materials employs large agitators that sweep the entire volume of the mixing vessel. Equipment intended to mix low viscosity liquids is typically equipped with an agitator that is small compared with the size of the vessel and depends upon turbulent flow for efficient mixing.

The fluid motion is the main focus of mixing it is the description of a single phase flow generated by one or more impellers inside a vessel and its characterization.

Macro-level mixing focuses on flow patterns, velocity profiles, velocity gradients, shear rates and distribution, turbulence spectrum, energy dissipation, pressure gradients, and impeller power consumption Many of these characteristics change with the flow regime, so understanding the effects of laminar, transitional, and turbulent flow regimes are important. Some processes are designed merely on the basis of its pumping capacity, its flow pattern, or the degree of shear produced. Without baffles, most impellers styles impose a tangential flow pattern. With baffles, most impellers show their true flow characteristics.

Baffles are needed to stop the swirl in a mixing tank. Almost all impellers rotate in the clockwise or counter-clockwise direction. Without baffles, the tangential velocities coming from any impeller(s) causes the entire fluid mass to spin. It may look good from the surface seeing that vortex all the way down to the impeller, but this is the worst kind of mixing. There is very little shear and the particles go around and around like in a Merry-Go-Round. This is more like a centrifuge than a mixer. Most common baffles are straight flat plates of metal that run along the straight side of vertically oriented cylindrical tank or vessel. This baffle design is often referred to as "standard baffles". There are many nuances. Some may have the baffles extend into the bottom dish or bottom head. Some may go up the straight side only partially (so-called partial baffles). Some baffles are flush with the side wall, but the majority has a space between the baffles and the tank's wall.

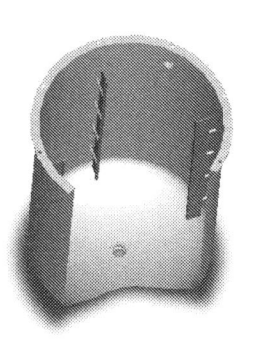

Most vessels will have at least three baffles. Four is most common and is often referred to as the "fully baffled" condition. This basically means that adding any more baffles doesn't significantly add to the power consumption of the impellers.

Baffle width, wB, is a function of the viscosity. For very high viscous fluids and broths, baffles are not even required, because there is enough resistance to flow at the walls. As the viscosity decreases, baffling becomes important and the baffle width gets larger.

In turbulent flows two standards of baffle widths have emerged: Metric standard (wB=1/10) and the American standard (wB=1/12). The difference is not large, but it is worth noting. Since the metric system is built on tenths, it is easy to determine baffle width. If the tank diameter, T, is 3 meters, then the baffle width is 300 mm.

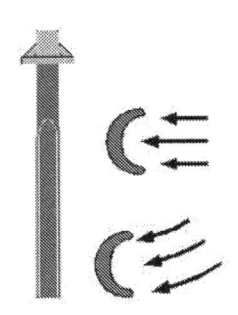

Most baffles start at the bottom tangent line of the lower head and run up to the top tangent line of the upper head. Some do extend down into the head. If you have consistent batch volumes or weights, it is best not to extend the baffles through the liquid surface, unless you want to entrain air into the batch. Baffles extending through the surface can create vortexes behind the baffles and entrain air. In viscous media, the baffles can create dead zones on the surface, and pack-up the material in front of the baffle (in flow direction). If you are adding sticky solids on the surface, the baffles are a great place for materials to agglomerate.

When axial flow down-pumping impellers are used, a crucifix baffle in the base may be all that is needed. The crucifix baffle is comprised of two plates that cross (usually in the center). They should not be placed directly on the bottom of the tank, so that solids don't get stuck.

A flat plate baffle in the outlet stream of a side-entry mixer can help to straighten the flow and reduce the formation of a vortex emitting from the impeller.

To design an agitation system - tank, shaft, impellers, and baffles (or baffle plate) - each component must be built strong enough to withstand the fluid forces generated by the impellers. Many calculations and programs are based on conservative hand-waving ideas based on the torque on the impeller shaft times some multiplier. [25]

INDUSTRIAL AND HOUSEHOLD BASE PRODUCT FORMULATIONS

This section covers basic industrial and household formulations which have been established to provide functional performance criteria in the appropriate industry. Theses base formulations include information on raw material percentage by weight or volume, key properties, and a description of the product. It is recommended that all formulations should be tested to maximize the performance of the product and to minimize material cost.

INDUSTRIAL CLEANER PRODUCTS

Hard Surface Cleaners

Description: Water soluble heavy duty cleaner for a wide variety of cleaning surfaces. This is a low phosphate formula designed for heavy soil and grime applications; the product keeps the soil in suspension for superior cleaning. By diluting the product a wide range of applications can be reformed with this product.

Applications: Kitchen, maintenance, repair shops, schools.

Usage: Dilutions from 1:3 to 1:30

Formula: Hard Surface Cleaner

Chemical	Weight percentage (Wt %)
Water	Balance
Sodium metasilicate	2.0 (+/- .5)
Potassium pyrophosphate	2.0(+/- .5)
Glycol Ether PnB	6.0(+/- 1)
Sodium Xylene Sulfonate (40%)	9.0(+/- 1)
Neodol 25-7 Linear Alcohol Ethoxylate	3.0(+/- .5)
Neodol 25-3 Linear Alcohol Ethoxylate	2.5(+/- .5)
Pine oil	.025

Chemical	Weight percentage (Wt %)
Water	Balance
Sodium metasilicate	2.0 (+/- .5)
Potassium pyrophosphate	2.0(+/- .5)
Glycol Ether PnB	4.0(+/- 1)
Sodium Xylene Sulfonate (40%)	7.0(+/- 1)
Tergitol 15-S-5 Nonylphenol Ethoxylate	2.0(+/- .5)

Chemical	Weight percentage (Wt %)
Water	Balance
Sodium metasilicate	2.0 (+/- .5)
Potassium pyrophosphate	2.0(+/- .5)
Glycol Ether PnB	6.0(+/- 1)
Sodium Xylene Sulfonate (40%)	4.0(+/- 1)
Witconate 1260 emulsifier	4.0(+/- .5)
Igepal CO-630 Nonylphenol Ethoxylate	7.5(+/- .5)

Chemical	Weight percentage (Wt %)
Water	Balance
Sodium metasilicate	2.0 (+/- .5)
Potassium pyrophosphate	4.0(+/- .5)
Glycol Ether PnB	4.0(+/- 1)
Sodium Xylene Sulfonate (40%)	6.0(+/- 1)
Witconate 1250 emulsifier	2.0(+/- .5)
Plurafac D-25 Nonionic Surfactant	2.0 (+/- .5)

Chemical	Weight percentage (Wt %)
Water	Balance
Sodium metasilicate	2.0 (+/- .5)
Potassium pyrophosphate	2.0(+/- .5)
Glycol Ether PnB	5.0(+/- 1)
Sodium Xylene Sulfonate (40%)	7.0(+/- 1)
Witconate 1250 emulsifier	3.0(+/- .5)
Plurafac D-25 Nonionic Surfactant	4.0 (+/- .5)
Plurafac RA-40 Nonionic Surfactant	2.5 (+/- .5)

Hard Surface Cleaners

Description: Water soluble heavy duty cleaner for a wide variety of cleaning surfaces. This is designed for heavy soil and grime applications.

Applications: Kitchen, maintenance, repair shops, schools.

Usage: Dilutions from 1:5 to 1:20

Formula: Hard Surface Cleaner

Chemical	Weight percentage (Wt %)
Water	Balance
Potassium pyrophosphate	3.0 (+/- 1)
Glycol Ether PnB	4.0 (+/- .5)
Neodol 91-6 Linear Alcohol Ethoxylate	4.0 (+/- .5)

General Purpose Cleaner

Description: Heavy duty cleaner for a wide variety of cleaning surfaces. This is a glycol ether based formula designed for heavy soil and grime applications; the product keeps the soil in suspension for superior cleaning. By diluting the product a wide range of applications can be reformed with this product.

Applications: Kitchen, maintenance, repair shops, schools.

Usage: Dilutions from 1:3 to 1:30

Formula: General Purpose Cleaner

Chemical	Weight percentage (Wt %)
Glycol Ether DPnB	10 (+/- 2)
Glycol Ether PnB	10.8 (+/- 2)
Pine oil	61.2 (balance)
Triethanolamine	7.2 (+/- 2)
Oleic Acid	10.8 (+/- 2)

Paint Brush Cleaner

Description: Cleaner for paint applications.

Applications: Home, business, maintenance, repair shops, schools.

Usage: As is.

Formula: Paint Brush Cleaner

Chemical	Weight percentage (Wt %)
Xylene	90 (Balance)
Glycol Ether PM	2.3 (+/- .5)
Glycol Ether DPM	2.6 (+/- .5)
Glycol Ether TPM	1.1 (+/- .4)
Miramine OC surfactant	4.0 (+/- 1)

All Purpose Cleaner

Description: Water soluble heavy duty cleaner for a wide variety of cleaning surfaces. This formula designed for general applications; the product keeps the soil in suspension for superior cleaning. By diluting the product a wide range of applications can be reformed with this product.

Applications: Home, office, maintenance, repair shops, tool and die shops and schools.

Usage: Dilutions from 1:3 to 1:20

Formula: General Cleaner

Chemical	Weight percentage (Wt %)
Water	Balance
Trisodium Phosphate	4.0 (+/- 1)
Glycol Ether PnB	4.0 (+/- 1)
Ninol 1285 Alkylolamide	3.0 (+/- 1)
Pine Oil	3.0 (+/- 1)
Sodium Xylene Sulfonate (40%)	7.0 (+/- 2)

Chemical	Weight percentage (Wt %)
Water	Balance
Sodium metasilicate	1.0 (+/- .5)
Sipex BOS Sulfate	3.0(+/- 1)
Siponic SK surfactant	2.0(+/- 1)
Glycol Ether PnB	10.0(+/- 2)
Sodium Xylene Sulfonate (40%)	5.0(+/- .5)
Monoethanolamine (MEA)	2.0 (+/- .5)

Chemical	Weight percentage (Wt %)
Water	Balance
Sodium metasilicate	1.0 (+/- .5)
Sipex BOS Sulfate	3.0(+/- 1)
Siponic SK surfactant	2.0(+/- 1)
Glycol Ether PnB	10.0(+/- 2)
Sodium Xylene Sulfonate (40%)	5.0(+/- .5)
Monoethanolamine (MEA)	2.0 (+/- .5)

Usage: Dilutions from 1:5 to 1:200

Chemical	Weight percentage (Wt %)
Miranol C2M-Sf Amphoteric	25.0 (+/- 5)
Alfonic 1012-40 additive (Ethoxylate)	13.0 (+/- 2)
Glycol Ether PnB	14.0 (+/- 2)
Mineral Spirits	45.0 (Balance)
Triethanolamine 85	3.0(+/- .5)

Usage: Dilutions from 1:3 to 1:20

Chemical	Weight percentage (Wt %)
Water	Balance
Sodium Carbonate	2.5 (+/- .5)
Versene 100 Chelating agent	2.0(+/- .5)
Sodium Xylene Sulfonate (40%)	4.0(+/- .8)
Glycol ether PnB	5.0(+/- 1)
Ethanol	1.5(+/- .5)
Tergitol 24-L-60 Surfactant	7.0 (+/- 1)

Chemical	Weight percentage (Wt %)
Water	Balance
Glycol Ether DPM	2.5 (+/- .5)
Glycol Ether DPnB	2.5 (+/- .5)
Sodium Carbonate	4.0 (+/- .8)

Neutral pH Cleaner

Description: This product is a mild, pH neutral cleaner (pH range 7.0 to 7.5). This product contains biodegradable surfactants and no phosphates. This product is a multi purpose cleaner that will not harm floor finishes or irritate skin. It is designed for general cleaning applications.

Applications: Linoleum floors, leather, plastic, vinyl upholstery, painted wall, ceramic, porcelain tile, tables and other furniture.

Usage: Dilutions from 1:20 to 1:100

Formula: Neutral pH Cleaner

Chemical	Wt % range
Water	Balance
Sodium hydroxide	1.5-1.2
Triethanolamine	1.0-0.5
Dodecylbenzene Sulfonic Acid	7.0-5.5
Surfonic N95	3.0-1.5
Surfamide M-1	6.0-5.0
Chelon 10 (EDTA)	0.8-0.3
Perfume (Formulators choice)	0.1
Dye (Color)	.001

Formula: Neutral pH Cleaner

Usage: Dilutions from 1:5 to 1:50

Chemical	Wt % range
Surfamide 81	40-30
Glycol Ether PnB	6.0-4.0
Water	Balance
Perfume(scent)	3.0-1.0

Chelon 10 (EDTA)	12.0-9.0
Glydant (antimicrobial)	1.5-0.9

Chemical	Wt % range
Surfonic N95	55.0-50.0
Tall Oil Fatty Acid	17.0-14.0
Glycol Ether EB	17.0-14.0
Propylene Glycol	6.0-4.0
Pluronic L-61	4.5-3.0
Water	Balance

Neutral pH Cleaner/Concentrate

Description: This product is a mild, pH neutral cleaner (pH range 7.0 to 7.5) is an economical cleaner concentrate. The cleaner can be applied to most cleaning applications, such as daily moping of floors. The product will not damage wax or acrylic finishes. This is a nontoxic, nonflammable product for most water washable surfaces.

Applications: Linoleum floors, plastics, wall water washable surfaces.

Usage: Dilutions from 1:15 to 1:100

Formula: Neutral pH Cleaner

Chemical	Wt % range
Water	Balance
Glycol Ether PnB	6.0-4.5
Surfamide 81	38.0-33.0
Chelon 100 (EDTA)	11.0-9.0
*Glydant (Dimethyl hydantoin)	1.5-0.8
Perfume	1.5-.09

*__Dimethyl hydantoin__ (DMH) is a versatile base molecule which can be derivatized and used for a number of functions such as: biocides, lubricants, coalescing agents, emulsifier, and emollients.

Acid Cleaner

Description: This product is designed for mineral, rust and scale removal from metal and painted surfaces, including water meters, process piping, swimming pools, masonry surfaces and plaster.

Applications: Water meters, radiators, metal surfaces, piping, concrete surfaces.

Usage: Dilutions from full concentrate to 1:10

Formula: Acid Cleaner

Chemical	Wt % range
Water	Balance
Hydrochloric Acid	65.0-55.0
Tergitol 15-S-12	1.0-0.5
Surfonic N-95	3.0-1.5
Dye (acid/water soluble)	0.8-0.1

Phosphoric Acid Cleaner

Description: This product is designed for removing hard water scale from dishwashing machines, steam tables, stainless steel, aluminum, and other metal surface.

Applications: Metal surfaces, dishwashing equipment, steam tables, concrete and brick, and acid resistant porcelain surfaces.

Usage: Dilutions from full concentrate to 1:5

Formula: Phosphoric Acid Cleaner

Chemical	Wt % range
Water	Balance
Dye (acid/water soluble)	1.0-0.2
Phosphoric Acid	55.0-50.0
Surfonic N-95	3.0-1.5

Ink Remover/Cleaner

Description: This product is designed for removing ink, crayon, lipstick and most spray paints.
Applications: Metal surfaces, ceramic tile, glass, and porcelain

Usage: As is.

Formula: Ink Remover/Cleaner

Chemical	Wt % range
Toluene	50.0-45.0
Trichlorethylene	48.0-40.0
Glycol Ether EB	6.0-4.0
Triton X-45	3.0-1.0

Paint and Varnish Cleaner/Remover

Description: This product is a blend of solvents and penetrating agents designed to remove paint and varnish.

Applications: Removes paint from cement surfaces, metal surfaces, floors, brick and furniture.

Usage: As is.

Formula: In Paint and Varnish Remover

Chemical	Wt % range
Methylene Chloride	19.0-18.0
Paraffin Wax	1.2-0.85

Step one: Mix until dissolved

Chemical	Wt % range
Methylene Chloride	70.0-60.0 (balance)
Hydroxypropyl methylcellulose	1.1-0.75
Methanol	6.0-4.8
Dye	1.0-0.5

Terpene Degreaser/Cleaner

Description: This product is a d-Limonene based cleaner. The product will remove heavy greases and oils form parts and equipment without harming most paints.

Applications: Part washing, equipment cleaning, adhesive remover, tar remover, and oil cleaner.

Usage: Dilutions from full concentrate to 1:20

Formula: d-Limonene Cleaner

Chemical	Wt % range
d-Limonene	95.0-90.0 (Balance)
Triton –X45	6.0-5.0
Surfonic N-95	3.0-1.5

Chemical	Wt % range
d-Limonene	60.0-48.0 (Balance)
Ninol 11 CM	50.0-35.0
Tomah E-14-5	12-.0-9.0

*Ninol 11CM: Fatty Alkanolamide, detergent

Terpene Based Drain Cleaner

Description: This product is a Limonene based cleaner for drains.

Applications: This product is used in grease trap, floor drains, and laundry drain applications

Usage: Dilutions from 1:1 to full concentrate.

Formula: Terpene Based Drain Cleaner

Chemical	Wt % range
Mineral Spirits	50.0-44.0
d-Limonene	50.-45.0 (Balance)
Triton –X45	3.0-1.5
Surfonic N-95	3.0-1.5

Drain Flush/Cleaner

Description: A polymer based product design to remove inorganic deposits in drains.

Applications: Used regular cleaning application and flushing, cleans piping, wells and basins.

Usage: Dilutions from ½ to 1 gallon per 100 gallons of water

Formula: Drain Flush/Cleaner

Chemical	Wt % range
Water	99.0-98.0
*Germaben II	0.2-0.08
Flocculent	1.0-0.5

*Germaben II contains:
Propylene glycol 56%
diazolidinyl urea 30%
methylparaben 11%
propylparaben 3

Terpene Degreaser/Cleaner Gel

Description: This product is a d-Limonene based cleaner. The product is a gel formulation that clings to surfaces to increase the performance of cleaning. The product also contains emulsifiers that bind with soils for easy removal.

Applications: Road construction equipment, metal surfaces, concrete floors engine blocks, frames and other auto application.

Usage: As is

Formula: Terpene Degreaser/Cleaner Gel

Chemical	Wt % range
d-Limonene	75.0-68.0 (balance)
Mineral Spirits	25.0-23.0
Polyalkylene Glycol (Pluronic)	3.0-2.0
Dye (orange color)	.01-.001
*Cabosil M-5	4.0-2.5
Ethylene Glycol	0.8-0.1

***Cabosil M-5** untreated fumed silica is a fine white synthetic amorphous colloidal silicon dioxide (similar to Gasil 23). It has an extremely small particle size of 0.2 to 0.3 microns.

Chlorinated Foam Cleaner

Description: Hypochlorite based cleaner, used for cutting grease and soils with addition of a foaming surfactant to solubilize the grease and soil.

Applications: Metal surfaces, dishwashing equipment, steam tables, concrete and brick, and acid resistant porcelain surfaces.

Usage: As is

Formula: Chlorinated Foam Cleaner

Chemical	Wt % range
Water	Balance
Sodium Tripolyphosphate	8.0-7.0
Potassium hydroxide	20.0-18.5
Sodium hypochlorite	16.0-15.5
Lauramine oxide	5.0-3.8

Silicone Cleaner

Description: This product is designed to clean and protect glass, tile, rubber, plastic, vinyl, leather, fiberglass, painted, and metal surfaces. This produce deposits a water repellent layer that keeps the surface clean and shiny.

Applications: Windows, doors, and bathroom surfaces.

Usage: As is

Formula: Silicone Cleaner

Chemical	Wt % range
Water	Balance
Surfonic N-95	0.3-0.2
Polydimethylsiloxane (T SIL SF-20)	1.5-1.0
Polydimethylsiloxane (T SIL SF-50)	3.0-2.0
*Germaben II-E	.01-.009

*__Germaben II-E__ is a solubilized combination of Germall II with methylparaben and propylparaben in propylene glycol. It is a complete broad spectrum antimicrobial preservative system that is effective against Gram-positive and Gram-negative bacteria and against yeast and mold.

Odor Control

Cleaner/Disinfectant/lemon scent

Description: This product is a disinfectant, deodorizer, and fungicide use for multiple surfaces.

Applications: Disinfectant, deodorizer, and fungicide for household and institutions.

Usage: Used at 2 oz/gallon.

Formula: Cleaner/Disinfectant lemon scent

Chemical	Wt % range
Water	Balance
Sodium Tripolyphosphate	3.5-2.8
*Quaternary Ammonium, Chlorine	6.0-5.5
Surfonic N-95	5.0-4.2
Perfume	.03-.005
Dye	.01-.001

*__Quaternary ammonium compounds__
Cetyl Quats have antistatic properties useful in a variety of personal care and industrial applications.
Product recommend for Cetyl Quats: Carsoquat® CT-429:
Carsoquat® CT-429
is used in hair care formulations, as hair conditioner, cream rinse and clear conditioner.
Dialkyl quats are a class of quaternary ammonium compounds generally used as disinfectants, sanitizers and algaecides. They are particularly effective against difficult to control organisms in hard water and in the presence of organic soil.
Product recommend for Dialkyl Quats: Bardac® 2080:
Bardac® 2080
is used as fungicide, bacteriostat, deodorizer, sanitizer, disinfectant.
Long chain ADBAC quats have antistatic and surface active properties useful in a variety of personal care and industrial applications.
Product recommend for Long chain ADBAC Quats: Uniquat® QAC-80:
Uniquat® QAC-80:
is a blend of alkyl dimethyl benzyl ammonium chlorides selected for performance as a cationic surfactant. It finds application in textile finishing, pulp and paper, sugar refining, water treatment, household and industrial cleaners.

Water based lemon scent

Description: This product is designed to control odor in sewage plants, lagoons, aerators, garbage and refuse containers.

Applications: Sewage plants, lagoons, aerators, garbage and refuse containers, haulers, dumps, sewer mains and laterals.

Usage: As is.

Formula: lemon scent

Chemical	Wt % range
Water	Balance
Surfonic N 95	6.0-5.0
Isopropyl Alcohol	6.0-5.0
Scent Lemon (Taylor 5006)	3.0-1.8
Dye (water soluble)	.01-.001

Water based Cherry scent

Description: This product is designed to control odor in sewage plants, lagoons, aerators, garbage and refuse containers.

Applications: Sewage plants, lagoons, aerators, garbage and refuse containers, haulers, dumps, sewer mains and laterals.

Usage: As is.

Formula: Cherry scent

Chemical	Wt % range
Water	Balance
*Ninol 11CM	1.5-0.5
Isopropyl Alcohol	3.0-2.0
Perfume Cherry (Geranyl butyrate)	1.0-.89
Dye	.01-.001

*Ninol 11CM: Fatty Alkanolamide, detergent

METAL CLEANER AND LUBRICTATING PRODUCTS

Aluminum cleaner

Description: Aluminum cleaner/brightener

Applications: Aluminum metal.

Usage: Dilutions from 1:1 to full concentrate.

Formula: Aluminum cleaner

Chemical	Weight percentage (Wt %)
Water	Balance
Phosphoric Acid (85%)	49.0-48.0
Igepal Co-630	11.0-10.0
Glycol Ether DPM	26.0-25.0
o-dichlorobenzene	5.0-3.5

Rust Remover/ Two Part Dip Application

Description: Metal cleaner

Applications: Rust and corrosion removal

Usage: As is.

Formula: Rust Remover

Part One

Chemical	Weight percentage (Wt %)
Water	Balance
Phosphoric Acid (85%)	32.0-29.0
Glycol Ether DPM	13.0-11.5
Triton X-100	0.5-.01

Part Two

Chemical	Weight percentage (Wt %)
Water	Balance
Phosphoric Acid (85%)	45.0-39.5

Glycol Ether DPM	11.0-9.5
Triton X-100	.02-.01

Rust Coating Converter

Description: This product chemical converts rust into an inert coating, the product neutralizes the rust, the formation and oxidation. The surface changes color to a black film producing a tough durable barrier

Applications: Rust formation

Usage: As is.

Formula: Rust Coating Converter

Part One

Chemical	Wt % range
Water	Balance
[1]Laponite RDS	0.8-0.7
[2]Colloid 646	0.3-.15
[3]Dowfax 2A1	0.3-0.15
[4]Surfynol 104 H	0.3-.02
[5]Kelzan S	0.3-0.2
[7]Polidene 37-0065	35.0-30.0
Tannic Acid	3.0-2.0

Part Two

Glycol Ether EB	3.0-1.5
[8]Polidene 37-0065	17.0-15.0

[1]**Laponite RDS**: Hydrous Sodium Lithium Magnesium Silicate with tetra sodium pyrophosphate
[2]**Colloid 646**: Liquid Defoamer
[3]**Dowfax 2A1**: Alkyldiphenyloxide Disulfonate
[4]**Surfynol 104 H**: 50% Surfynol 104 y 50% Etilen Glicol. (Surfynol 104: y 2, 4, 7, 9 - Tetrametil - 5 -Decin - 4, 7 - Diol.)
[5]**Kelzan S**: Xanthan Gum
[7]**Polidene 37-0065:** Aqueous emulsion of a vinylidene chloride copolymer

Metal Cleaner/ Coil Applications

Description: This product is an acid based cleaner form removal of soil, oil film, dust, scale, oxidation and corrosion from aluminum or air coils systems.

Applications: Copper, brass, and aluminum coils and heat exchangers.

Usage: Dilutions from 1:10

Formula: Metal Cleaner

Chemical	Wt % range
Water	Balance
Ammonium bifluoride	1.5-0.5
Surfonic N-95	3.0-1.5
Glycol Ether EB	5.0-4.0
Phosphoric Acid (85%)	26.0-24.0
Dye	.01-.001

Metal Surface Cleaner

Description: This product is an acid based cleaner form removal of soil, oil film, dust, scale, oxidation and corrosion from aluminum, ferrous, and galvanized metal surfaces.

Applications: Aluminum, ferrous, and galvanized metal surfaces.

Usage: As is.

Formula: Metal Cleaner

Chemical	Wt % range
Water	Balance
Phosphoric Acid	30.0-25.0
Glycol Ether EB	4.0-3.0

Metal Cleaner/ Aluminum

Description: This product is an acid based cleaner form removal of soil, oil film, dust, scale, oxidation and corrosion from aluminum surfaces.

Applications: Aluminum metal.

Usage: Dilutions from 1:10

Formula: Aluminum Cleaner

Chemical	Wt % range
Water	Balance
Disodium Capryloampho Diacetate	4.0-2.5
Sulfuric Acid (50%)	30.0-28.0
Hydrofluoric acid (70%)	11.0-9.0

Lubricating Oil

Description: This product penetrates, lubricate, protects, displaces, and seal out moisture and protects against rust.

Applications: Lubrication of equipment, waterproofing ignition systems and terminal, penetrating and loosening rust parts and protecting metal.

Usage: As is

Formula: Lubricating Oil

Chemical	Wt % range
140 Solvent(Aliphatic solvent)	Balance
*Alox 2028	13.0-11.0

ALOX 2028 — Nonstaining, alkali resistant, water separating, barium based
ADDCO CP-OB-1 — Low odor, light color, containing, barium based
ADDCO CP-OB-2 — Low odor, light color, nonstaining, calcium based
ALOX 165 — Nonstaining, alkali resistant, water separating, calcium based
ALOX 165L — Liquid non-emulsifiable, nonstaining, water separating
ALOX 168 — Nonstaining, alkali resistant, water-separating, calcium based
ALOX 1727D — Nonstaining slushing oil additive
ALOX 1937 — Nonstaining slushing oil additive
ALOX 2148 — Oxidized wax corrosion inhibitor
ALOX 2162 — Thin-film, limited salt spray rust preventive
ALOX 2211Y — Firm film, light colored, high melt point, thixotropic rust preventive
ALOX 2213A — Limited salt spray, water displacing, oil and solvent based
ALOX 2213C — Limited salt spray, water displacing, oil and solvent based
ALOX 2213D — Non-emulsifiable, limited salt spray, nonstaining, oil and solvent based
ALOX 2263 — Emulsifiable, barium-based, salt spray protection of phosphate and steel surfaces
ALOX 2280 — Emulsifiable soluble-oil corrosion inhibitor
ALOX 2289 — Acid fume inhibitor
ALOX 2290/2290A — Oil-soluble corrosion inhibitors, salt spray protection

ALOX 2291 — Barium sulfonate, high molecular weight
ALOX 2293 — High molecular weight sodium sulfonate
ALOX 2296 — Nonstaining, excellent humidity protection, oil-based
ALOX 318F — Acid fume inhibitor for solvent based systems
ALOX 319F — Acid fume inhibitor for solvent based systems
ALOX 575 — Barium based, oil, solvent emulsifiable, salt spray protection
ALOX 606 Series — Hard film, calcium soap, long-term outdoor protection
ALOXCOAT WB 706 — Water-based, hard clear film, humidity cabinet protection
AQUALOX 2320 — Emulsifiable, penetrating, humidity and salt spray protection and lubricity
AQUALOX 2328 — Emulsifiable wax, nonstaining, ferrous and nonferrous protection and lubricity
AQUALOX 2268 — Emulsifiable wax, salt spray on phosphate, lubricity
Calcium Sulfonate 10S and 55 — Oil-soluble synthetic calcium sulfonates

Penetrating Oil

Description: This product penetrates, lubricates and loosens frozen rusted parts and protects metal surfaces from corrosion.

Applications: Metal parts

Usage: As is

Formula: Penetrating Oil

Chemical	Wt % range
Trichloroethylene	35.0-32.0
Teflon Dispersion (Zonyl 7950)	1.4-1.1
Lard Oil #2	16.0-14.0
Nocco 100 oil #100-S	52.0-49.0

Coolant and Lubrication Fluid

Description: This product is for coolant/lubrication applications for cutting, turning, and all metal machining operations.

Applications: Metal parts: aluminum, zinc, copper, and other soft metals.

Usage: Dilution range 1:10 to 1:30

Formula: Coolant and Lubrication Fluid

Chemical	Wt % range
Water	Balance
*Fluent Lub or Ucon Fluid Lub	16.0-14.0
Hostacar BS (corrosion inhibitor)	11.0-9.0
Triethanolamine	7.0-5.8

*Fluent-Lub 309
Fluent-Lub 325
Fluent-Lub 344
Fluent-Lub 351
Fluent-Lub 397
UCON Fluid: polyalkylene glycol (PAG)-based synthetic products
LB Fluids are alcohol-started base stocks featuring oxypropylene groups (m=0) with one terminal hydroxyl group. They are water insoluble and available in a variety of molecular weights and viscosities.
50-HB Fluids are alcohol-started base stocks containing equal weight amounts of oxyethylene and oxypropylene groups with a single terminal hydroxyl group. They are water soluble at ambient temperature and are available in a variety of molecular weights and viscosities.
75-H Fluids are diol-started base stocks containing 75 weight percent oxyethylene and 25 percent oxypropylene groups with two terminal hydroxyl groups. They are water soluble at temperatures below 75°C and are available in a variety of molecular weights and viscosities.

Silicone Lubricant

Description: Silicone lubricant formulated to perform on a wide variety of applications

Applications: Eliminates metal to metal noise, rubber squeaks, lubricate hinges and prevents freezing of locks.

Usage: As is.

Formula: Silicone Lubricant

Chemical	Wt % range
Trichloroethylene	Balance
*Viscasil 60M	5.0-4.5

*Viscasil 60M: GE Silicone/Detergent antifoam

Industrial Degreaser

Description: High power degreaser

Applications: General applications

Usage: As is.

Formula: Industrial Degreaser

Chemical	Wt % range
KEROSENE	Balance
Glycol Ether DPM	16.0-14.0
Siponic SK	26.0-24.0

Spray Degreaser

Description: High power degreaser

Applications: General applications

Usage: As is.

Formula: Industrial Degreaser

Chemical	Wt % range
Water	Balance
Miranol C2M	4.0-2.0
Sodium Tripolyphosphate	2.0-1.0
Sodium Metasilicate	3.0-2.0
Trisodium phosphate	2.0-1.0
Tall oil fatty acid	2.0-1.0
Potassium Hydroxide (45%)	1.5-0.09
Glycol Ether PM	9.0-8.0

Steam Line Corrosion Inhibitor

Description: This is a neutralizing amine based formula to provide corrosion protection in stem condensate systems.

Applications: Regular usage for pH adjustment for untreated steam condensate in high and low pressure systems- designed to prevent acid formation.

Usage: Dosage varies depending on the size of the system

Formula: Steam Line Corrosion Inhibitor

Chemical	Wt % range
Water	Balance
Diethanolamine	5.5-4.9
Cyclohexylamine	5.5-4.9
UCON Fluid (5100)	0.9-.04

HOUSEHOLD CLEANING PRODUCTS

The following formulas have not been registered with the EPA (Environmental Protection Agency), formulations that you might choose to market with germicidal, disinfectant type claims must be registered with the EPA as required by the Federal Insecticide, Fungicide and Rodenticide Act (FIFRA).

Bathroom cleaner

Description: Bathroom Cleaner

Applications: Bathroom surfaces.

Usage: As is.

Formula: Bathroom cleaner

Chemical	Weight percentage (Wt %)
Water	Balance
Glycol Ether DPM	4.5-3.5
DOWICIDE A1 antimicrobial	0.6-0.4
DOWFAX 2A1	1.0-0.85
Versene 100	6.0-5.0
Versene Acid	0.4-0.28

Liquid Soap

Description: Liquid Soap

Applications: Cleaning.

Usage: As is.

Formula: Soap

Chemical	Weight percentage (Wt %)
Water	Balance
Potassium Hydroxide	5.5-4.5
Oleic Acid	21.0-19.5
Glycerin	21.0-19.0
Glycol Ether DPM	6.0-4.5

Liquid Hand Cleaner

Description: Liquid Hand Soap

Applications: Cleaning.

Usage: As is.

Formula: Hand Soap

Chemical	Weight percentage (Wt %)
Monoethanolamine	6.0-5.0
Oleic Acid	24.0-22.0
[1]Permethyl 99A	16.0-14.0
[2]Permethyl 101A	16.0-14.0
Glycol Ether DPM	Balance
Glycerin	16.0-14.5
Water	8.0-6.0

[1]Permethyl 99A (Presperse) (Isododecane)
[2]Permethyl 1012A (Presperse) (Isoeicosane)

Germicidal Disinfectant

Description: Bathroom Disinfectant

Applications: Cleaning.

Usage: Dilution range 1:10

Formula: Disinfectant

Chemical	Weight percentage (Wt %)
DOWICIDE 1	3.0-1.5
Glycol Ether DPM	11.0-9.5
DOWFAX 2A1	1.5-0.9
Sodium dodecyl benzene sulfonic acid	1.2-0.95
Water	Balance

Tile and Shower Cleaner

Description: This product is a foaming acid cleaner for removing soap scum, dirt, and scale.

Applications: Bathroom surface.

Usage: As is

Formula: Tile and Shower Cleaner

Chemical	Wt % range
Water	Balance
[1]Kelzan S	0.18-0.11
Sulfamic Acid	4.0-3.2
Hydroxyacetic Acid 70%	6.0-4.8
[2]Monateric CA-35	4.0-2.9
Isopropyl Alcohol	3.0-1.8
Perfume	0.02-0.01
Dye	0.1-0.01

[2]Masoteric is an active disodium coco imadozoline dicarboxylate surfactant in Water, multi-functional amphoteric surfactant characterized by
hydrolytic stability, detergency, and its ability to couple nonionic surfactants into strongelectrolyte solutions.
[1]Kelzan S: Xanthan Gum

Glass Cleaner

Description: This product is formulated for cleaning windows, mirrors, windshields, and other non porous surfaces such as chrome, stainless steel, ceramic tile and vinyl.

Applications: Glass and metal surfaces.

Usage: As is

Formula: Glass Cleaner

Chemical	Wt % range
Water	Balance
Glycol Ether PM	1.5-0.9
Glycol Ether EB	4.0-2.5
Isopropyl Alcohol	5.0-3.5

Surfonic N-95	0.18-0.09
Dye	.002-.001
Ammonium hydroxide	0.18-0.12

Formula: Glass Cleaner II

Chemical	Wt % range
Water	Balance
Glycol Ether DPM	6.0-4.0
Glycol Ether PM	6.0-4.0
Pluronic F 108	0.15-0.09
Colloidal Silica	5.0-3.0
Duponol C	0.06-0.04

Formula: All Purpose Glass Cleaner

Chemical	Wt % range
Water	Balance
Ammonium hydroxide (28%)	3.0-2.0
Pluronic L-10	0.2-0.09
Glycol Ether PnB	6.0-4.0

Formula: All Purpose Glass Cleaner II

Chemical	Wt % range
Water	Balance
Duponol C	0.06-0.04
Glycol Ether PnB	4.0-2.0
Glycol Ether DPnB	3.0-1.0
Pluronic L-10	0.2-0.09
Colloidal Silica	4.0-2.0

Formula: All Purpose Glass Cleaner III

Chemical	Wt % range
Water	Balance
Glycol Ether PM	6.0-4.0
Propylene Glycol	6.0-4.0
Isopropanol	40.0-30.0

Formula: All Purpose Glass Cleaner IV

Chemical	Wt % range
Water	Balance
Glycol Ether PM	9.0-7.0
Ammonium Hydroxide	2.0-1.0
Pluronic F108	0.2-0.09

Formula: Windshield Washer

Chemical	Wt % range
Water	Balance
Glycol Ether PM	17.0-15.0
Glycol Ether DPM	7.0-5.0
Pluronic L-62	0.03-0.01

Formula: Windshield Washer II

Chemical	Wt % range
Water	Balance
Glycol Ether PM	6.0-4.0
Glycol Ether DPM	6.0-4.0
Colloidal Silica	5.0-3.0
DOWFAX 2A1	0.06-0.04

Ultra Glass Cleaner Concentrate

Description: This product is formulated for cleaning windows, mirrors, windshields, and other non porous surfaces such as chrome, stainless steel, ceramic tile and vinyl.

Applications: Glass and metal surfaces.

Usage: Dilution range 1:10 to 1:50

Formula: Ultra Glass Cleaner Concentrate

Chemical	Wt % range
Water	Balance
Tetra potassium pyrophosphate	6.0-4.0

Sodium Xylene Sulfonate (40%)	11.0-9.0
Glycol Ether EB	22.0-19.0
Sodium Laureth Sulfonate	15.0-13.0
Dye	0.1-0.001

Organic Bowl Cleaner

Description: This product is formulated to dissolve stubborn deposits and rust stains from porcelain and chrome

Applications: Toilet Bowl Cleaner.

Usage: As is

Formula: Toilet Bowl Cleaner.

Chemical	Wt % range
Water	Balance
Surfonic N-95	0.2-0.09
Sulfamic Acid	16.0-15.0
Malic Acid	6.0-4.8
Citric Acid	4.0-2.9
Kelzan S	0.8-0.6
Perfume (Clean scent)	0.01-.009
Dye	0.01-0.001

Acidic Bowl Cleaner

Description: This product is formulated to dissolve stubborn deposits and rust stains from porcelain and chrome

Applications: Toilet Bowl Cleaner.

Usage: As is

Formula: Toilet Bowl Cleaner.

Chemical	Wt % range
Water	Balance
Hydrochloric Acid	70.0-50.0
Surfonic N-95	3.0-1.0

*Polyrad 515	2.0-0.5
Dye	0.1-0.001

*POLYRAD® AMINE CORROSION INHIBITOR, imidazoline corrosion inhibitor

Disinfectant Sanitizer

Description: Quaternary ammonium compound

Applications: General application.

Usage: As is
Formula: Disinfectant Sanitizer

Chemical	Wt % range
Water	Balance
*Maquat (Quaternary ammonium)	13.0-12.0

*Maquat® BPGTMC
Maquat® BTMC-35%
Maquat® BTMC-85%
Maquat® C-15
Maquat® C-15MS
Maquat PQ-125
Maquat® CETAC-30%
Maquat® SC1632
Maquat® SC18
Maquat® QSX
Maquat® SL-5

Lemon Scent Disinfectant Sanitizer

Description: Quaternary ammonium compound

Applications: General application.

Usage: As is

Formula: Disinfectant Sanitizer

Chemical	Wt % range
Water	Balance
*Maquat (Quaternary ammonium)	6.0-5.2
Sodium Carbonate	4.0-2.0

Chemical	Wt % range
Chelon 100	3.0-2.0
Surfonic N-95	5.0-4.2
Lemon Scent	0.2-0.09
Dye (Yellow color)	0.1-0.001

*Maquat® BPGTMC
Maquat® BTMC-35%
Maquat® BTMC-85%
Maquat® C-15
Maquat® C-15MS
Maquat PQ-125
Maquat® CETAC-30%
Maquat® SC1632
Maquat® SC18
Maquat® QSX
Maquat® SL-5

Deodorizer Concentrate

Description: Multipurpose deodorizer that effectively eliminates odors from air conditioning ducts, toilets and urinals, floors and sink drains, carpets and furniture.

Applications: General application.

Usage: Dilution range 1:10 to 1:100

Formula: Deodorizer Concentrate

Chemical	Wt % range
Water	Balance
Phosphate Ester (monafax)	2.0-1.0
Triethanolamine	1.5-0.9
Sodium Sulfate	0.30-0.02
Surfonic N-95	4.0-2.0
Propylene Glycol	3.0-1.5
Perfume	3.0-2.0
Dye	0.1-0.01

Non-Acid Bathroom Cleaner

Description: Bathroom applications such as sinks, shower stalls, and fixtures. Formulated for all surfaces including chrome and stainless steel. Removes soap scum, scale and lime deposits.

Applications: Bathroom surfaces.

Usage: As is.

Formula: Non-Acid Bathroom Cleaner

Chemical	Wt % range
Water	Balance
Sodium Laureth Sulfonate	2.0-1.0
Sodium tripolyphosphate	4.0-3.0
Chelon 100	6.0-4.9
Perfume	0.1-.008
Dye	0.1-0.01
DOWICIDE 1	0.2-0.09

Non-Acid Bathroom Cleaner II

Description: Bathroom applications such as sinks, shower stalls, and fixtures. Formulated for all surfaces including chrome and stainless steel. Removes soap scum, scale and lime deposits.

Applications: Bathroom surfaces.

Usage: Dilution range 1:10

Formula: Non-Acid Bathroom Cleaner

Chemical	Wt % range
Water	Balance
Sodium Laureth Sulfate	18.0-15.0
Sodium Metasilicate5 Hydrate	6.0-4.0
Chelon 100	6.0-4.0
DOWICIDE 1	2.0-0.9
Dye	0.1-0.001
Perfume	0.2-0.09

Grill Cleaner

Description: Removes heavily encrusted grease and carbon from ovens, grills, smokehouses.

Applications: Grease and carbon removal applications.

Usage: As is.

Formula: Grill Cleaner

Chemical	Wt % range
Water	Balance
Sodium tripolyphosphate	4.0-2.0
Sodium Metasilicate 5 Hydrate	4.0-2.0
Potassium Hydroxide	11.0-9.0
Glycol Ether EB	4.0-2.0
Surfamide 81	3.0-1.5
Sodium Laureth Sulfate	4.0-2.0
Dye	0.1-0.001

Hand Dishwashing Concentrate

Description: Heavy duty detergent for hand washing application such as pot and pans, flatware, glassware and silverware.

Applications: Kitchen applications

Usage: ¼ oz level usage, 1/2 to 1 once /gallon for heavy grease.

Formula: Hand Dishwashing Concentrate

Chemical	Wt % range
Water	Balance
Sodium Hydroxide	5.0-4.0
Dodecyl Benzene Sulfonic Acid	18.0-16.0
Chelon 100	0.5-0.1
Surfamide M-1	3.0-2.0
Sodium Laureth Sulfate	11.0-10.0
DOWICIDE 1	0.1-0.09
Perfume	0.8-0.2

Alkaline Cleaner and Degreaser

Description: Removes grime, oil and grease from metal, concrete, and painted surfaces.

Applications: High temperature steam cleaner

Usage: Dilution from 1:20 to 1:40.

Formula: Alkaline Cleaner and Degreaser

Chemical	Wt % range
Water	Balance
Sodium tripolyphosphate	6.0-4.0
Sodium Metasilicate 5 Hydrate	9.0-7.0
Sodium Laureth Sulfate	4.0-2.0
Potassium Hydroxide	4.0-2.0
Dye	0.1-0.001

Daily Shower Cleaner

Description: Cleans shower surfaces, removes scale and soap scum.

Applications: Shower surfaces

Usage: As is

Formula: Daily Shower Cleaner

Chemical	Wt % range
Water	Balance
Chelon 100	5.0-3.0
Chelon 120	4.0-2.0
Neodol 1-7	0.2-0.1
Isopropyl Alcohol	3.0-1.0
Citric Acid	0.8-0.1
Perfume	0.03-0.01

RUG, CARPET AND FLOOR CARE PRODUCTS

Rug and Carpet Cleaner

Description: Cleans heavy soil, grease and stains from carpet fibers, rugs and upholstery.

Applications: Carpet, rug and upholstery.

Usage: As is

Formula: Rug and Carpet Cleaner

Chemical	Wt % range
Water	Balance
Trisodium Phosphate	3.0-1.0
*Orvus K	8.0-6.0
Glycol Ether PnB	6.0-4.0

*Orvus K: sodium dodecyl sulfate

Rug and Carpet Cleaner, Low Foam

Description: Cleans heavy soil, grease and stains from carpet fibers, rugs and upholstery.

Applications: Carpet, rug and upholstery.

Usage: As is

Formula: Rug and Carpet Cleaner, Low Foam

Chemical	Wt % range
Water	Balance
DOWFAX 2A1	8.0-6.0
Triethanolamine	12.0-9.0
Glycol Ether PM	5.0-3.5
Potassium Oleate	2.0-0.5

Rug and Carpet Cleaner, Medium Foam

Description: Cleans heavy soil, grease and stains from carpet fibers, rugs and upholstery.

Applications: Carpet, rug and upholstery.

Usage: As is

Formula: Rug and Carpet Cleaner, Medium Foam

Chemical	Wt % range
Water	Balance
Glycol Ether DPM	6.0-4.0
Trisodium Phosphate	3.0-1.0
Sodium dodecyl sulfate	8.0-6.0

Liquid Steam Cleaner

Description: Cleans heavy soil, grease and stains from carpet fibers, rugs and upholstery.

Applications: Carpet, rug and upholstery cleaning equipment.

Usage: As is

Formula: Liquid Steam Cleaner

Chemical	Wt % range
Water	Balance
Chelon 100	4.0-2.0
Sodium orthosilicate	5.0-4.0
Ninol 1285	12.0-10.0
Glycol Ether PnB	6.0-4.0

Carpet Anti Stat

Description: Eliminates static charge from rugs, carpets, upholstery and other areas which static builds

Applications: Carpet, rug and upholstery applications.

Usage: As is

Formula: Carpet Anti Stat

Chemical	Wt % range
Water	Balance
*Larostat 264A	3.0-2.0
Isopropyl Alcohol	9.0-7.0

*LAROSTAT® 264 A: QUATERNARY AMMONIUM COMPOUND

Spot and Stain Remover

Description: Eliminates heavy soil, grease and stains from carpet and rugs.

Applications: Carpet and rug applications.

Usage: As is

Formula: Spot and Stain Remover

Chemical	Wt % range
Water	Balance
Neodol 1-7	2.0-1.0
Neodol 1-3	1.0-.05
d-Limonene	2.0-1.0
Isopropyl Alcohol	6.0-4.0
Sodium Meta pyrophosphate	4.0-2.0
Sodium dodecyl sulfate	3.0-1.0

Solvent Carpet Cleaner

Description: Spot treatment for heavy soil, grease and stains from carpet, rugs and upholstery.

Applications: Carpet, rug and upholstery.

Usage: As is

Formula: Solvent Carpet Cleaner

Chemical	Wt % range
Odorless Mineral Spirits	Balance
Trichloroethylene	42.0-39.5
Surfonic N-95	3.0-1.5

High Traffic Carpet Cleaner

Description: Treatment for heavy soil, grease and stains from carpet and rugs for high traffic areas.

Applications: Carpet and rug applications.

Usage: As is

Formula: High Traffic Carpet Cleaner

Chemical	Wt % range
Water	Balance
Trisodium Phosphate	1.0-0.3
Sodium tripolyphosphate	1.5-0.5
Sodium Metasilicate	1.5-0.5
Chelon 100	0.9-0.1
Dodecylbenzene Sulfonic Acid	2.0-1.0
Sodium Hydroxide	0.7-0.5
Glycol Ether EB	7.0-6.0
Dye	0.1-0.001

Low Foam Extractor Cleaner

Description: Removes embedded dirt and soil, cleans fibers and raises the nap, for both steam and hot water extractors.

Applications: Carpet and rug applications.

Usage: As is

Formula: Low Foam Extractor Cleaner

Chemical	Wt % range
Water	Balance
Tertapotassium pyrophosphate	4.0-3.0
Chelon 100	0.9-0.4
Amphoteric	13.0-12.0
Sulfo-Ester	6.0-5.0
Dye	0.1-.001

Powder Extractor Cleaner

Description: Removes embedded dirt and soil, cleans fibers and raises the nap, for both steam and hot water extractors.

Applications: Carpet and rug applications.

Usage: As is

Formula: Powder Extractor Cleaner

Chemical	Wt % range
Sodium Triypolyphosphate	22.0-18.0
Sodium Carbonate	22.0-18.0
[1]Polytergent SLF-18	12.0-9.0
Sodium Sulfate	4.0-3.0
[2]Tinopal CBS -X	50.0-45.0
Perfume	0.1-0.001

[2]Tinopal CBS-X: Brightener
[1]Polytergent SLF-18 BASF

Spot and Stain Remover

Description: Eliminates heavy soil, grease and stains from carpet and rugs.

Applications: Carpet and rug applications.

Usage: As is

Formula: Spot and Stain Remover

Chemical	Wt % range
Water	Balance
Sodium Hydroxide	5.0-3.0
Glycol Ether DPM	13.0-11.0
Triethanolamine	11.0-9.0
Oleic Acid	50.-46.0
Perchloroethylene	22.0-19.0

Spot and Stain Remover II

Description: Eliminates heavy soil, grease and stains from carpet and rugs.

Applications: Carpet and rug applications.

Usage: As is

Formula: Spot and Stain Remover II

Chemical	Wt % range
VM&P Naptha	Balance
Igepal CO-630	2.0-1.0
Glycol Ether DPM	16.0-15.0
Isopropanol	14.0-12.0
Perchloroethylene	32.0-18.0

Floor Cleaner

Description: Eliminates heavy soil, grease and stains from most floor tile and vinyl surfaces.

Applications: Floor applications.

Usage: As is

Formula: Floor Cleaner

Chemical	Wt % range
Glycol Ether PM	15.0-13.0
Trisodium Phosphate	13.0-11.0
Triton X-100	17.0-15.0
Water	Balance

Floor Cleaner II

Description: Eliminates heavy soil, grease and stains from most floor tile and vinyl surfaces.

Applications: Floor applications.

Usage: As is

Formula: Floor Cleaner II

Chemical	Wt % range
Glycol Ether PM	15.0-13.0
Water	Balance
Oleic Acid	17.0-15.0
Triethanolamine	13.0-11.0

Wax Stripper

Description: Product is designed for easy removal of all types of floor finishes.

Applications: Floor applications.

Usage: As is

Formula: Wax Stripper

Chemical	Wt % range
Glycol Ether PM	9.0-7.0
Trisodium Phosphate	3.0-2.0

Triton X-100	9.0-7.0
Water	Balance

Wax Stripper II

Description: Product is designed for easy removal of all types of floor finishes.

Applications: Floor applications.

Usage: As is

Formula: Wax Stripper II

Chemical	Wt % range
Glycol Ether PM	15.0-13.0
Ammonium hydroxide	7.0-6.0
*Niaproof 08	5.0-4.0
Water	Balance

*NIAPROOF 08, sodium ethylhexyl sulfate

Wax Stripper III

Description: Product is designed for easy removal of all types of floor finishes.

Applications: Floor applications.

Usage: As is

Formula: Wax Stripper III

Chemical	Wt % range
Water	Balance
Trisodium Phosphate	3.0-2.0
Glycol Ether PnB	9.0-7.0
Triton x-102	9.0-8.0

Floor Seal

Description: This product is a water repellent, oil and stain resistant seal to protect wood floors.

Applications: Floor applications.

Usage: As is

Formula: Floor Seal

Chemical	Wt % range
Mineral Spirits	Balance
*ESI-CYRL 4100	45.0-44.0
**ESI-CYRL 645	15.0-13.0
N-Butanol	0.3-0.2
DOWICIDE 1	0.8-0.5
9% Manganese NuXtra drier	0.07-0.05
Exkin#2(antiskinning agent)	0.2-0.012

ESI-CYRL
*ESI-CRYL™ 4100
ESI-CRYL™ 43N40
ESI-CRYL™ 4000
ESI-CRYL™ 325N35
**ESI-CRYL™ 645
ESI-CRYL™ RT239
ESI-CRYL™ 2540N
ESI-CRYL™ 54N35
ESI-CRYL™ 629N38
ESI-CRYL™ 2988
ESI-CRYL™ 625N
ESI-CRYL™ 4435

Floor Finish

Description: This product is a water repellent, oil and stain resistant finish to protect wood floors.

Applications: Floor applications.

Usage: As is

Formula: Floor Seal

Chemical	Wt % range
Mineral Spirits	Balance
*ESI-CYRL 4100	60.0-55.0
**ESI-CYRL 645	20.-19.0
N-Butanol	0.5-0.3
DOWICIDE 1	0.09-0.07
9% Manganese NuXtra drier	0.1-0.05
Exkin#2(antiskinning agent)	0.2-0.15

ESI-CYRL
*ESI-CRYL™ 4100
ESI-CRYL™ 43N40
ESI-CRYL™ 4000
ESI-CRYL™ 325N35
**ESI-CRYL™ 645
ESI-CRYL™ RT239
ESI-CRYL™ 2540N
ESI-CRYL™ 54N35
ESI-CRYL™ 629N38
ESI-CRYL™ 2988
ESI-CRYL™ 625N
ESI-CRYL™ 4435

AUTOMOTIVE CARE PRODUCTS

Car Wash concentrate

Description: For all types of vehicles, removes dirt and leave spot free surface

Applications: Automotive

Usage: Dilute from 1:10 to 1:100

Formula: Car Wash Cleaner

Chemical	Wt % range
Water	Balance
Surfonic N-95	7.0-5.0
Monafax 1293	10.0-8.0
Sodium Metasilicate 5 Hydrate	7.0-5.0
Chelon 100	40.0-25.0

Car Polish and Sealer

Description: For all types of vehicles, provides high gloss and long lasting surface.

Applications: Automotive

Usage: As is

Formula: Car Polish and Sealer

Chemical	Wt % range
Water	Balance
Carbopol 941	0.35-0.20
d-Limonene	3.0-2.0
WAX emulsion	11.0-9.0
Morpholine	2.0-1.0
DOWICIDE 1	0.1-0.09
Viscasil 10M	2.0-0.9
Silicone Fluid 18-350	5.0-3.0
Oleic Acid	2.0-1.0
Silicone Fluid SF	2.0-1.0
Isopar-m	7.0-5.0

| *Kaopolite 1152 | 7.0-5.0 |

*Kaopolite 1152: aluminum; tetrahydroxysilane; hydrate

Car Wash and Wax

Description: For all types of vehicles, cleans dirt and grime while adding a protective coating to the surface.

Applications: Automotive

Usage: As is

Formula: Car Wash and Wax

Chemical	Wt % range
Water	Balance
Surfonic N-95	5.0-3.0
Cocoamidopropyl Betaine	4.0-2.0
Emulsifier 4	4.0-2.0
Dye	0.1-.001

Car Wax

Description: For all types of vehicles, water beading agent

Applications: Automotive

Usage: As is

Formula: Car Wax

Chemical	Wt % range
Mineral Seal Oil	25.0-19.5
Emulsifier 4	16.0-15.0
Glycol Ether EB	4.0-2.0
Water	Balance 62.0-59.0
Surfonic N-95	0.85-0.65

Car Foam

Description: For all types of vehicles, a high foaming detergent concentrate.

Applications: Automotive

Usage: 1 to 6 oz per gallon

Formula: Car Foam

Chemical	Wt % range
Water	Balance
Sodium tripolyphosphate	5.0-3.0
Potassium Hydroxide	3.0-2.0
Dodecylbenzene Sulfonic Acid	8.0-7.0
Sodium Laureth Sulfate	9.0-7.0
Surfamide M-1	2.0-1.5
DOWICIDE 1	0.3-0.15
Perfume	0.09-0.05

Silicone Polymer and Cleaner

Description: Designed for providing a long lasting coating which repels dirt and dust. This product is for plastic, vinyl, leather, rubber and also similar surfaces.

Applications: Automotive, for plastic, vinyl, leather, rubber surfaces.

Usage: As is

Formula: Silicone Polymer and Cleaner

Chemical	Wt % range
Water	Balance
Surfonic N-95	2.0-0.9
Silicone Emulsion SM 2163*	15.0-14.0
Silicone Emulsion SM 2059	2.0-1.0
DOWICIDE 1	0.1-0.05

* Similar products: Synonyms: GE SM 2163, GE 2163, Dow Corning 346 Emulsion, DC 346, silicone emulsion, 60% silicone emulsion, water-based silicone, water - soluble silicone, non-flammable silicone lubricant

Silicone Emulsion SM 2059 is a reactive emulsion of an amine functional silicone polymer in water. This product cures to an elastomeric film without the need of a catalyst.

Asphalt and Tar Remover

Description: Designed to penetrate and soften deposits from road construction materials roofing tools and equipment.

Applications: Automotive surfaces

Usage: As is or diluted up to 8 parts of the following solvents:

Kerosene
Mineral Spirits
Fuel Oil

Formula: Asphalt and Tar Remover

Chemical	Wt % range
Monochlorotoluene	Balance
*Toximul D-A	2.0-0.5
*Toximul H-A	2.0-0.5

Toximul: SULFONATE/NONIONIC SURFACTANT BLEND: General agricultural emulsifier: Solubility Xylene

Windshield Washer/Deicer

Description: Designed for providing quick ice, snow, and frost removal.

Applications: Automotive windshield.

Usage: As is

Formula: Windshield Washer/Deicer

Chemical	Wt % range
Isopropyl Alcohol	Balance
Methanol	4.0-2.0
Glycol Ether EB	4.0-2.0
Water	16.0-14.0
Surfonic N-95	0.09-0.01

Engine Cleaner and Degreaser

Description: Designed for removing grim and grease from metal surfaces.

Applications: Automotive.
Usage: As is

Formula: Engine Cleaner and Degreaser

Chemical	Wt % range
Water	Balance
Monoisopropanolamine	21.0-19.0
Surfonic N-95	4.0-2.0
Glycol Ether DPM	16.0-14.0
Chelon 100	3.0-1.0

Heavy Oil and Grease Remover

Description: Designed for removing grim and grease from metal surfaces.

Applications: Automotive.

Usage: As is

Formula: Heavy Oil and Grease Remover

Chemical	Wt % range
Xylene	Balance
Perchloroethylene	35.0-29.0
Igepal CO-530	21.0-18.0
Glycol Ether DPM	21.0-19.0

Whitewall Tire cleaner

Description: Water based heavy duty detergent for cleaning tire whitewalls.

Applications: Automotive.

Usage: As is

Formula: Whitewall Tire cleaner

Chemical	Wt % range
Water	Balance
Miranol CM emulsifier	21.0-18.0
Sodium Metasilicate	28.0-26.0
Glycol Ether PM	3.0-1.5
Potassium Hydroxide	4.0-2.5

Whitewall Tire cleaner II

Description: Water based heavy duty detergent for cleaning tire whitewalls.

Applications: Automotive.

Usage: As is

Formula: Whitewall Tire cleaner II

Chemical	Wt % range
Water	Balance
Glycol Ether PnB	7.0-5.0
*Ninol 11CM	0.8-0.5
*Ninol 1281	0.5-0.4
Stepanate SODIUM XYLENE SULFONATE	0.5-0.4
Witconate K (Na DDBSA)	2.0-0.9
Chelon 100	4.0-2.0
Sodium o-silicate	0.2-0.09

*Ninol: FATTY ALKANOLAMIDE, DETERGENT GRADE
Product Application Emulifiers and lubricants with antistatic properties for textiles. Water soluble/dispersible emulsifiers and corrosion inhibitor.

Heavy Duty Truck Cleaner

Description: Water based heavy duty detergent for cleaning heavy soils, grease and dirt from vehicle.

Applications: Automotive.

Usage: As is

Formula: Heavy Duty Truck Cleaner

Chemical	Wt % range
Water	Balance
*Sipex BOS sulfate	5.0-3.0
Siponic L-12	3.0-1.0
Siponic 218	7.0-5.0
Glycol Ether DPM	5.0-3.0
Sodium Xylene Sulfonate	4.0-2.0
Sodium Metasilicate	2.0-0.5
Chelon 100	2.0-1.0

*Sipex BOS: SODIUM DODECYL SULFATE, Alcolac Inc.

Leather, Vinyl and Plastic Cleaner

Description: Designed for providing a long lasting coating which repels dirt and dust. This product is for plastic, vinyl, leather, rubber and also similar surfaces.

Applications: Automotive, for plastic, vinyl, leather, rubber surfaces.

Usage: As is

Formula: Leather, Vinyl and Plastic Cleaner

Chemical	Wt % range
Water	Balance
Igepal CO-630	12.0-9.0
Glycol Ether PM	6.0-4.0
Isopropanol	3.0-2.0
Amyl Acetate	1.8-0.9

Appendix: Chemical Formulation Information

General Chemical List

2
2-Ethyl Hexanol
2-Ethyl Hexoic Acid

A
Absorbent, Oil
Accosoft Fabric Softners
Acesulfame K
Acetic Acid
Acetic Anhydride
Acetone
Acid Cleaners
Acid Fiber Reactive
Acid Inhibitors
Acids - ACS, Reagent, Technical
Acidulants
Acintene Terpine Solvts
Acintol Fatty Acids
Acintol Tall Oil
ACL's
Acrawax®
Activated Alumina
Activated Carbon
Adipic Acid
Aerosol OT®
Aircraft Deicing Fluid
Alcohol Ethoxylates
Alcohols
Algaecides
Alkalies
Alkaline Cleaners
Alkanolamides
Alkanolamine
Alkanols
Alkyl Ether Sulfates
Alkyl Sulfates
Alkylaryl Sulfonate
Alox Surfactants
Alpha-Step Surfactants
Alum, Activated
Alum, Ground
Alum, Iron free
Alum, Liquid
Alum, Potassium
Alum, Rice
Aluminopolysilicates
Aluminum Chloride Solution

M
Machine Way Lubricants
Magnesium Bisulfite, Liquid
Magnesium Carbonate
Magnesium Chloride
Magnesium Hydroxide
Magnesium Oxide
Magnesium Stearate
Magnesium Sulfate
Magnifloc®
Maleic Anhydride
Malic Acid
Mallinckrodt/Baker Reagents
Maltodextrine
Manganese Sulfate
Mannitol
Manual Cleaner
Marine Lubricants
Mazer Surfactants
MCC
McGean Rohco Product Line
M-Clene-D®
Melamine
Merpols
Metal Cleaners - Acid, Alkaline, Solvent
Metal Preservative Oil
Metal Working Fluid
Metals Anodes & Salts
Metasilicate
Methanol
Methyl Amyl Acetate
Methyl Amyl Alcohol
Methyl Carbitol™
Methyl Cellosolve Acetate
Methyl Cellosolve™
Methyl Chloroform
Methyl Ethyl Ketone
Methyl Isoamyl Ketone
Methyl Isobutyl Carbinol
Methyl Isobutyl Ketone
Methyl Methacrylate
Methyl Paraben
Methyl Propasol Acetate
Methyl Propasol Solvent
Methyl Salicylate
Methylene Chloride
Methylparaben

Aluminum Chlorohydrate
Aluminum Etchants
Aluminum Pigments
Aluminum Stearate
Aluminum Sulfate
Ambitrol
Amine Oxides
Amines
Amino Acids
Aminoacetic Acid, "Glycine"
Aminoethylethanolamine
Ammonia Alum
Ammonia, Anhydrous
Ammonia, Aqua
Ammonium Acetate
Ammonium Aluminum Sulfate
Ammonium Bicarbonate
Ammonium Bifluoride
Ammonium Bisulfite, Liquid
Ammonium Carbonate
Ammonium Chloride
Ammonium Fluoborate
Ammonium Hydroxide
Ammonium Lauryl Ether Sulfate
Ammonium Lauryl Sulfate
Ammonium Lauryl Sulfonate
Ammonium Molybdate
Ammonium Nitrate
Ammonium Pentaborate
Ammonium Persulfate
Ammonium Phosphates
Ammonium Silicofluoride
Ammonium Sulfamate
Ammonium Sulfate
Ammonium Thiocyanate
Ammonium Thiosulfate
Ammonium Xylene Sulfonate
AMP-95
Amphoteric®
Amyl Acetate, HB & Primary
Amyl Alcohol
Anhydrous Ammonia
Anodes
Anodes, Metal
Anodizing Chemicals
Anti-Foam
Antifreeze
Anti-Stat
Aqua CeI
Aqua Nuchar
Arcosolv®
Arklone Solvents

Microcel
Microcrystalline Wax
Military Spec Product
Mineral Oil
Mineral Seal Oil
Mineral Spirits
Minex Pigments
Minfoam®
Minspar Pigments
Mixed Acids
Molecular Sieves
Molten Salts
Mono- & Diglycerides
Monoammonium Phosphate
Monocalcium Phosphate
Monochlorobenzene
Monochlorotoluene
Monodiethanolamine
Monoethanolamine
Monoethylamine 70%
Monoisopropanolamine
Monopotassium Phosphate
Monosodium Phosphate
Mop Oil
Morlex®
Morpholine
Motor Oil
M-Pyrol®
MSG
Multiwaxe®
Muriate Of Potash
Muriatic Acid

N

N,N' Ethylenebisstearamide
Nacconol Products
Nalan®
Naphtha - Aliphatic & Aromatic
Naphthenic Oil
Napthol Spirits
Natural Gas Engine Oil
Natural Oil
N-C-Plus
Neodol®
Neutral Oil
Nickel Acetate
Nickel Anodes
Nickel Brightener
Nickel Carbonate
Nickel Chloride (Dry & Liquid)
Nickel Fluoborate
Nickel Sulfamate

Aromatic 100 & 150
Ascorbic Acid
Aspartame
Asphalt Additives
Asphalt Emulsifiers
Asphalt Removers
ATF Fluids
Automotive Lubes
Aviation Grease
Aviation Oil
Avitex®
Axarel™

B

B Carotene
Bacteriocide
Bardac®
Barium Carbonate
Barium Chloride
Barlox®
Barquat®
Barytes
Base Oils
Basic Oil Soluble
Battery Acid
Bentone Clay
Benzalkonium Chloride (BTC 50 USP)
Benzoflex Plasticizers
Benzoic Acid
Benzyl Alcohol
Benzyl Chloride
Betaines
BHA/BHT
Bilge Cleaners
Biosoft, Bioterge Detergent Intermediates
Biosoft, Bioterge, BTC, Ninol, Stepanol, Stepanate (Stepan Co.)
Blanket Washes
Bleach
Blends
Borax (All Grades)
Boric Acid (All Grades)
Bottle Wash Compounds, Liq. & Dry
Brass Anodes
Brass Oxidizers
Brighteners
Briquest Polyphosphonates
Briquest™
BTC Quats

Nickel Sulfate
Nickel Sulfate, Single Salts
Nickel, SC Chips & Rounds
Nigrosines®
Ninol Surfactants
Niterox®
Nitric Acid
N-Methyl Pyrrolidone (NMP)
Non-Chromate Deoxidizers
Non-Cyanide Plating System
Nonyl Phenol
Novamax Products
N-Propyl Acetate
N-Propyl Alcohol
NTA®

O

Odorless Mineral Spirits
Oil & Fuel Additives
Oils, Lubricating
Oils, Specialty
Oleic Acid
Oleum
Organic Titanates
Organophosphates
Orthodichlorobenzene
Orthotolidine
Orvus®
Outboard/2 Cycle Oil
Oxalic Acid
Oxone®
Oxsol™
Ozene

P

Paint Additives
Paint Removers
Paint Strippers
Paint Thinners
Pale Oil
Parabens
Paradichlorobenzene
Paraffin Wax, Food Grade
Paraffinic Oil
Paraformaldehyde
Parolite®
Pectin
Pegosperse®
Peladow™
Perchlorethylene
Persulfates
Petro AA, BA, BAF, ULF, S, 22, Udet

Buffing Compound Removers
Burco Products (Burlington Chemical)
Butanediol
Butyl Acetate
Butyl Alcohol, Normal & Secondary
Butyl Carbitol
Butyl Carbitol Acetate
Butyl Cellosolve Acetate™
Butyl Cellosolve™
Butyl Stearate
Butylated Hydroxy Toluene
BYK Paint Additives

C

Cadmium Anodes
Caffeine
Calamide®
Calcium Ascorbate
Calcium Carbonate
Calcium Chloride (Liq., Powder, Flake, Pellets)
Calcium Chloride, Hi-Test
Calcium Formate
Calcium Hypochlorite
Calcium Nitrate
Calcium Phosphates
Calcium Propionate
Calcium Saccharin
Calcium Silicate
Calcium Stearate
Calfax®
Calfoam®
Calibrating Fluids
Calsoft®
Calsuds®
Capryl Alcohol
Caramel Color
Carbitol Acetate™
Carbitol Solvent™
Carbon Disulfide
Carbon Tetrachloride
Carbon, Activated
Carbons
Carbowax®
Carboxymethylcellulose, Sodium Salt
Carob Bean Gum
Carrageenan Gum
Casein, Special Grades
Castor Oil, Sulfonated

(Witco Inc.)
Petro Surfactants
Petrolatum (White USP & Tech, all grades)
Petroleum Ether
Petroleum Sufonate
Pharmaceutical Specialties
Phenol
Phenol Glycol Ether
Phenol Red
Phosphate Cleaner
Phosphate Ester Acid
Phosphates
Phosphates Full line of Food Phosphates
Phosphonates
Phosphoric Acid
Phthalates
Phthalic Anhydride
Pigments
Pine Oil
Pine Oils, Arizole
Plasticizers
Plating Chemicals
Polyaluminum Chloride
Polyethylene Glycol Esters
Polyethylene Glycols
Polyethylenes
Polymers, Detergent & Specialty
Polyol Esters
Polyols
Polypropylene Glycols
Poly-Solv's
Polysorbates
Polysorbates, Sorbitan Esters
Poly-Tergent®
Polyvinyl Alcohol
Potassium Copper Cyanide Doublesalts
Potassium Acetate
Potassium Acid Tartrate
Potassium Alum
Potassium Benzoate
Potassium Bichromate
Potassium Carbonate
Potassium Chloride
Potassium Chromate
Potassium Citrate
Potassium Copper Cyanide
Potassium Cyanide
Potassium Fluoborate
Potassium Fluoride, Reagent
Potassium Gluconate
Potassium Hydroxide

Catalyzed Sulftech (Sodium Sulfite)
Caustic Potash (Flake, Liquid)
Caustic Soda
Caustic Soda (Flake, Liquid, Beads)
CDB Clearon®
CELATOM® Filter Media
Celatom® SP
Celite® Fillers
Celite® Filters
Cellosolve Acetate
Cellosolve Solvent
Ceramic Support Media
Cetrimonium Chloride (Ammonyx)
Cetyl Alcohol
Chain Conveyor Lubricants
Chelating Agents
CHEM-Films
Chlor
Chloride Agents
Chlorinated Solvents
Chlorine Gas
Chloroform
Chrome Plating
Chromic Acid
Citric Acid
Citrosol®
CKWitco Silicone Antifoams
Clay, Kleen-sorb
Clays
CMC
Coagulant Aids
Cobalt Compounds
Cocamide DEA (Ninol)
Cocamidopropyl Amine Oxide (Ammonyx)
Cocamidopropyl Betaine (Amphosol)
Coconut Diethanolamides
Colloidal Silicas
Compressor Oil
Concrete Form Oil
Conversion Coatings
Cooling, Recirculating, Potable & Waste Water Treatment Chemicals
Copper & Brass Bright Dips
Copper Anodes
Copper Carbonate
Copper Cyanide
Copper Fluoborate
Copper Metal

Potassium Iodide
Potassium Metabisulfite
Potassium Monopersulfate
Potassium Nitrate
Potassium Nitrite
Potassium Permanganate
Potassium Persulfate
Potassium Phosphates
Potassium Silicate
Potassium Silicofluoride
Potassium Sodium Tartrate
Potassium Sorbate
Potassium Stannate
Potassium Sulfate
Potassium Tetraborate
Potassium Tripolyphosphate
Precofloc
Preservative Oil
Preservatives
Press & Blanket Wash
Prestochlor Calcium Hypochlorite, (Granular & Tablet)
Prestoline Products
Primary Amyl Acetate
Primary Amyl Alcohol
Printing Solvent
Process Oil
Propaklone Solvent
Propasol Solvents, B & R
Propionates
Propionic Acid
Propyl Acetate
Propyl Alcohol
Propyl Cellosolve™
Propyl Paraben
Propylene Carbonate
Propylene Glycol
Propylene Glycol USP
Propylene Glycol- USP
Pumice
Pyridoxine (B-6)

Q
Quadrafos®
Quaternary Ammonium Compound
Quenching Oil

R
R & O Lubricants
Railroad Lubricants
Reagent Grade Products
Refrigeration Oil

Copper Sulfate (All Grades)
Copperas
Corn Syrup Solids
Corrosion Preventives
Cosmetic ingredients, full line
Cream of Tartar
Cresols
Cupric Chloride
Custom Blended Thinners
Custom Blends
Custom Formulating, Liquid & Dry
Cyanide Double Salts
Cyanides
Cyanuric Acid
Cyclohexane
Cyclohexanol
Cyclohexanone
Cyclohexylamine
Cyclosolv 53, 63
Cylinder Oils

D
DDBSA
Defoamers
Degreasing Solvents
Deionized Water
Denatured Alcohols
Deoxidizers/Desmutters
Dequest Polypyhosphonates, 2000,2010 series
Dequest®
Derusters/Descalers
Detergent Builders, Emusifiers, Surfactants, Polymers & Thickeners
Detergents - Anionic, Nonionic, Alkyl Sulfates
Developers Spirit Soluble
Dextrose
Dextrose Cerelose
Di (Hydrogenated) Tallow Phthalic Acid Amide (Stepan TAB-2)
Diacetone Alcohol
Diammonium Phosphate
Diatomaceous Earth
Dibasic Ester
Dibutyl Phthalate
Dicalcium Phosphates
Dicyanadiamide
Dielectric Oil
Dielectric Solvent
Diesel Engine Lubes

Resins, Escorez
Riboflavin (B-2)
Rochelle Salts
Roller Wash
Roof, Floor & Shingle Oil
Rubber Solvent
Rust Preventative
Rust Proof Oil

S
Safety Solvents
Salicylic Acid
Salt - Epsom, Glauber, Rochelle,
Salt Cake
Saniticizers
Sarcosine Acid
Sarcosine Acids, Hamposyl C, O, L, M
Semi Conductor Chemicals
Sequesterants
Sequestrene®
Silanes
Silicates
Silicon Dioxide
Silicones (complete range)
Snowflake, Crystals
Soak Cleaners
Soaps
Soda Ash
Soda Ash (Briquettes, Dense, Light)
Sodium Acetate
Sodium Acid Pyrophosphate
Sodium Aluminate, Solution
Sodium Aluminosilicate
Sodium Ascorbate
Sodium Benzoate
Sodium Bicarbonate
Sodium Bichromate
Sodium Bifluoride
Sodium Bisufate
Sodium Bisulfite (All Types)
Sodium C12-15 Alkoxypropyl Iminodipropionate (Tomah Amphoteric N)
Sodium C14-16 Olefin Sulfonate (Bioterge AS-40)
Sodium Carbonate Monohydrate
Sodium Chlorate
Sodium Chloride (All Types)
Sodium Chlorite, Liquid & Dry
Sodium Chromate, Technical & Anhy.
Sodium Citrate
Sodium Copper Cyanide

Diethanolamine
Diethyl Phthalate
Diethylamine
Diethylene Glycol
Diethylene Glycol Monobutyl Ether
Diethylene Glycol Monoethyl Ether
Diethylene Glycol Monomethyl Ether
Diethylenetriamine
Diethylethanolamine
Diethylformamide
Diglycolamine
Diisobutyl Ketone
Diisodecyl Phthalate
Diisopropylamine
Dimer Acid
Dimethyl Acetamide
Dimethyl Phthalate
Dimethylethanolamine
Dimethylformamide
Dioctyl Adipate
Dioctyl Phthalate
Dioxane 1,4
Dipentine
Dipotassium Phosphate
Dipropylene Glycol
Discolites®
Disodium Phosphate
Dispersants, full line
Distilled Water
Dizene®
D-Limonene
Dober Product Lines
Dodecylbenzenesulfonic Acid
Dowanols®
Dowflake™
Dowfrost™
Dowtherm™
Drawing Oil
Dry Chlorine
Dry Cleaning Solvent
Duozinc®
Duponols®
Durad Lubricants
Dust Suppressants

E
EDM Fluid
EDTA
EDTA products
EEH, EEP, EP Solvents

Sodium Copper Cyanide Double Salts
Sodium Cyanide, Brick & Granular
Sodium Cyclomate
Sodium Dimethyldithiocarbanate
Sodium Dodecylbenzene Sulfonate
Sodium Erythorbate
Sodium Fluoride
Sodium Formate
Sodium Glucoheptonate (Liq. & Crystals)
Sodium Gluconate
Sodium Hexametaphosphate
Sodium Hydrosulfide
Sodium Hydrosulfite
Sodium Hydroxide
Sodium Hypochlorite
Sodium Hypophospite
Sodium Hyposulfite
Sodium Laureth Sulfate (Steol)
Sodium Lauryl Ether Sulfate
Sodium Lauryl Sarcosinate (Hamposyl)
Sodium Lauryl Sulfate
Sodium Lauryl Sulfoacetate (Lathanol)
Sodium Metabisufite
Sodium Metasilicate
Sodium Molybdate, Anhy. & Dihy.
Sodium Nitrate
Sodium Nitrite
Sodium Orthosilicate
Sodium Perborate
Sodium Percarbonate
Sodium Percarbonate (FB)
Sodium Peroxide
Sodium Persulfate
Sodium Phosphate (All Types)
Sodium Polyacrylates
Sodium Propionate
Sodium Saccharin
Sodium Sesquicarbonate
Sodium Silicate (All Grades)
Sodium Silicofluoride
Sodium Stannate
Sodium Sulfate
Sodium Sulfhydrate
Sodium Sulfide
Sodium Sulfite
Sodium Sulphoxylate Formaldehyde
Sodium Tetrasulfide
Sodium Thiocyanate
Sodium Thiosulfate
Sodium Tripolyphosphate
Sodium Tungstate

Electro Cleaners
Electrolyte
Electronic Chemicals
Emulsifiers
Emulsion Cleaners
Engine Chassis Degreasers
Enzymes, Burco Detergent Specialties
Epoxy Resins & Curing Agents
Epsom Salt, Technical & USP
Erythorbic Acid
Ethyl Acetate
Ethyl Alcohol -Pure
Ethyl Alcohol- SDA
Ethyl Alcohols, Denatured
Ethyl Amyl Ketone
Ethyl Ether
Ethyl Paraben
Ethyl Vanillin
Ethylene Carbonate
Ethylene Diamine
Ethylene Dichloride
Ethylene Glycol
Ethylene Glycol Monobutyl Ether & Acetate
Ethylene Glycol Monoethyl Ether
Ethylene Glycol Monomethyl Ether & Acetate
Ethylene Oxides, Amine Condensates
Ethylene/Propylene Carbonate
Ethylenediamine
Etidronate (Briquest)

F

Fabric Softeners, Accosoft
Fatty Acids
Feldspar Pigments
Ferric Ammonium Oxalate
Ferric Chloride
Ferric Sulfate
Ferri-Floc®
Ferrous Chloride
Ferrous Sulfate
Fidelity Products
Filter Aids
Finnfix®
Fire Resistant Lubricants
Firebrake® ZB
Fish Oil
Flame Retardants
Flocculants

Sodium Xylene Sulfonate
Sodiurn Hypochlorite, Saniticizer and Cleaner
Softeners (Fabric, Water)
Sol 71
Soluble Oil
Solvent 142 HT
Solvent Blends
Solvent Emulsion Cleaners
Solvents - Alcohols, Aliphatic, Aromatic, Chlorinated, Custom Blended, Freon®, Fluorinated, 140, 360, etc.
Sorbic Acid
Sorbistat®
Sorbitan Esters
Sorbitan Monostearate
Sorbitol
Soy Bean Oil - Epoxidized
Soya Lecithin
Specific Gravity Fluids
Spindle Oil
Spray Gun Cleaner
Stannochlor™
Stannous Chloride
Stannous Fluoborate
Stannous Methanesulfonate
Stannous Oxide
Stannous Sulfate
Stearates
Stearic Acid
Stearyl Alcohol
Steol Product
Stepan Surfactants
Stepanates
Stoddard Solvent
Styrene
Sucrose
Sulfamic Acid
Sulfonates
Sulfonic Acid
Sulframin Beads®
Sulfur (All Types)
Sulfur Dioxide
Sulfuric Acid
Surfactants
Surfonic NP, L series (Texaco Chemical)
Surfonic®
Swimming Pool Chemicals
SXS 40%
Symbol Oils (Milspec)
Synthetic Lubricants

Floor Absorbents
Floor Dri®
Fluoborates
Fluoboric Acid
Fluorocarbon Solvent
Fluorosurfactants
Fluorspar
Flux Removers
Fluxes
Foam Suppressants
Folic Acid
Food Freeze®
Food Grade Chemicals
Food Machinery Lubes
Form Oils
Formaldehyde
Formic Acid
Fragrances for Industrial Products
& Odor Masks
Freon®
Fructose
Fumaric Acid
Fume Suppressants
Fumed Silica
Furfural
Furfuryl Alcohol

G

Galvanizing Fluxes
Gas Treating Amines
Gear Oil
General Purpose Cleaners
Genesolv® Solvent
Gilsonite
Glauber Salt
Gluconic Acid
Glucono Delta Lactone
Glycerine
Glycerine USP
Glycerol Esters
Glycol Ether Alternatives
Glycol Ethers
Glycolic Acid
Glycols
Glycolube®
Glycomul®
Glycosperse®
Gold Dye for Anodized Aluminum
Graphic Cleaners
Greases, all types
Grinding Oil
Guar Gum

T

Talc
Tall Oil
Tallow & Tallow Amines
Tannic Acid
Tartar Emetic
Tartaric Acid
TEA Dodecylbenzene Sullonate
Terathane®
Tergitol®
Terpene Solvents, Acitene DP 738
Terpine Resin
Tetraethylene Glycol
Tetrahydrofuran
Tetrahydrofurfuryl Alcohol
Tetrapotassium Pyrophosphate
Tetrasodium Pyrophosphate
Texanol®
Textile Lubricants
Textile Specialties
Textone®
Textreat® Products
Thiamine Hydrochloride
Thiamine Mononitrate
Thiourea
Thiourea Dioxide
Tin Anodes
Tin Fluoborate
Tin-Lead Anodes
Tinopal®
Titanium Dioxide
Toluene
Tolusol 5
Tomah Products - Application Chemicals
Torque Fluid
Transformer Oil
Transmission Gear Lube
Tri Calcium Phosphate
Tributoxy Ethyl Phosphate
Tributyl Phosphate
Tributyl Phthalate
Tricalcium Phosphates
Trichloro (ISO) Cyanuric Acid
Trichlorobenzene
Trichloroethane 1.1.1
Trichloroethylene
Tricresyl Phosphate
Triethanolamine
Triethanolamine Lauryl Sulfate
Triethylamine
Triethylene Glycol
Triethylene Tetramine

Gum Arabic
Gum Tragacanth

H
Halso 99®
Hampenes®
Hamposyls, C, L, O, M C-30, L-30
(Hampshire Chemical Corp.)
Heat Transfer Fluids
Heavy Aromatic Naphtha
Henkel Paint Additives
Heptane
Hexamethylenetetramine®
Hexamine
Hexane
Hexylene Glycol
Hi Flash Naphtha
High Temp Greases
Honing Oil
HTH®
Humectants
Hydrated Lime
Hydraulic Oils
Hydrazine
Hydrochloric Acid
Hydrofluoric Acid
Hydrofluosilicic Acid
Hydrogen Peroxide
Hydrogen Peroxide F.G.
Hydrogen Peroxide Stabilizer
Hydroquinone
Hydrotropes, Detergent
Hydrous Polysilicates
Hydroxyacetic (Glycolic)Acid
Hydroxyecetic Acid
Hyflo Super Cel®
Hypophosphorous Acid

I
Imidazoline Amphoterics
Inhibited Acids
Inhibitors
Ink Solvents
Ink Thinners
Inorganic Chemicals
Inositol
Insulating Oils
Iodophor Germicides
Iron Chloride
Iron Phosphates
Isoamyl Alcohol
Isobutyl Acetate

Triethyltriamine
Triphenyl Phosphate
Triphenyl Phosphite
Tripotassium Phosphate
Tripropylene Glycol
Trisodium Phosphate, (Crystal & Anhy.)
Trisodium Phosphate, chlorinated
TriStar NF® Tabletting Lubricant
Triton®
Tufflo®
Tung Oil
Turbine Cleaning Oil
Turpentine, gum
Turpentine, steam distilled
TXIB Plasticizer
Type Wash
Tyzor®

U
UCAR® Filmer IBT®
UCAR® Food Freeze
UCAR® PM Acetate
UCAR® PM Solvent
UCAR® Thermofluid®
Ucon Heat Transfer Fluid®
Urea
Uvitex®

V
Vanillin
Vanishing Oil
Various Thinners
Varsol®
Vatrolite®
Versene Acid®
Versene®
Versenex ™
Versenol®
Vertrel®
Vicron
Virtex®
Vitamins B12, D2, D3, E
VM&P Naphtha

W
Water Treatment Chemicals
Watercarb®
West Clean Front, Low Foam series,
Iodophors (West Agro, Inc.)
Wetting Agents
White Oil

Isobutyl Alcohol
Isobutyl Carbinol
Isopar®
Isophorone
Isophthalic Acid
Isopropyl Acetate
Isopropyl Alcohol
Isopropyl Alcohol- USP
Isopropyl Ether
Isopropyl Myristate (KESSCO IPM)
Isopropyl Palmitate (KESSCO IPP)
Isopropylamine
Ivory Beads®

J
Jet Engine Oil

K
K-1 Kerosene
Kasil®
Kenite
Kerosene Odorless
Kerosene, deodorized
KESSSCO Esters
Ketones
Kjell Aqua Mag
Knitting Oil
KP-140 Plasticizer
Kronitex®

L
Lacquer Diluent
Lacquer Thinner
Lacquer Washes
Lactic Acid
Lactol Spirits
Lanolin
LAS-99®
Lead Fluoborate
Lecithin
Lime, Hydrated
Lime, Pebble
Lime, Quick Pulverized
Linseed Oil
Liquid Prestochlor
Locust Bean Gum
Lonzaines®
Low VOC Solvents
Lubricants/Oils
Ludox®

Wire Rope Lubricant
Witsol PD (refined aliphatic)

X
Xanthan Gum
Xylene

Y
Yelkin Products

Z
Zaclon®
Zelec®
Zeolite aluminopolysilicates, Detergent Grade
Zinc Ammonium Chloride
Zinc Anodes
Zinc Borate
Zinc Chelated Agricultural Micronutrients (Hampene)
ZInc Chloride
Zinc Cyanide
Zinc Dust
Zinc Fluoborate
Zinc Hydrosulfite
Zinc Nitrate
Zinc Oxide
Zinc Stearate
Zinc Sulfate
Zinc Sulfoxylate
Zinc Sulfoxylate Formaldehyde
Zonyl®
Zorball®

Solubility

Solubility of Common inorganic compounds in grams solute per 100 mL of water						
Substance	0°C	10°C	20°C	30°C	40°C	50°C
KI, potassium iodide	127.5	136	144	152	160	168
KCl, potassium chloride	27.6	31.0	34.0	37.0	40.0	42.6
NaCl, sodium chloride	35.7	35.8	36.0	36.3	36.6	37.0
$NaHCO_3$, sodium bicarbonate	6.9	8.15	9.6	11.1	12.7	14.45
NaOH, sodium hydroxide	--	--	109	119	145	174
$MgSO_4 \cdot 7 H_2O$, Epsom salts magnesium sulfate heptahydrate	--	23.6	26.2	29	31.3	--

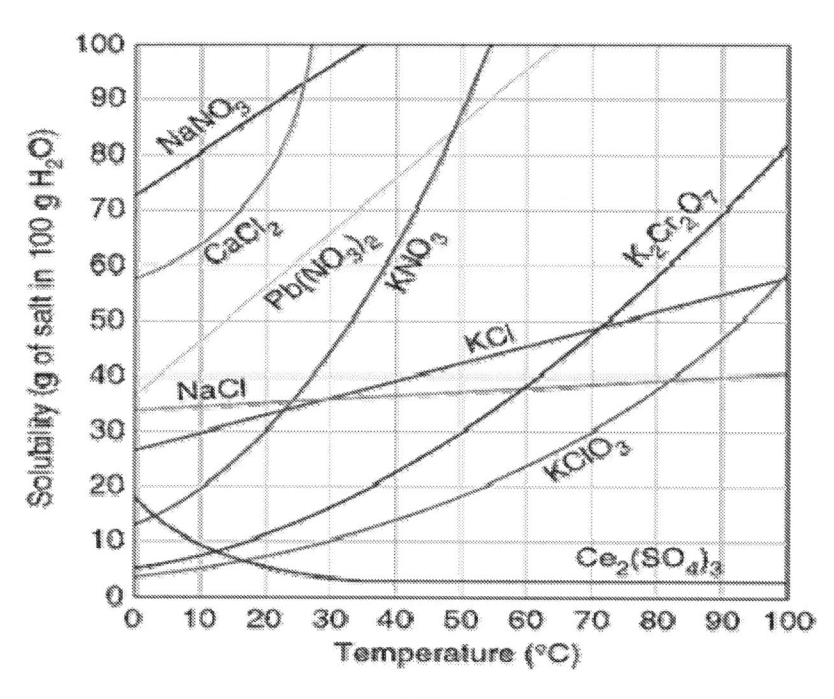

SOLUBILITY PRODUCT CONSTANTS

Compound	Formula	K_{sp} (25 °C)
Aluminum hydroxide	$Al(OH)_3$	3×10^{-34}
Aluminum phosphate	$AlPO_4$	9.84×10^{-21}
Barium bromate	$Ba(BrO_3)_2$	2.43×10^{-4}
Barium carbonate	$BaCO_3$	2.58×10^{-9}
Barium chromate	$BaCrO_4$	1.17×10^{-10}
Barium fluoride	BaF_2	1.84×10^{-7}
Barium hydroxide octahydrate	$Ba(OH)_2 \times 8H_2O$	2.55×10^{-4}
Barium iodate	$Ba(IO_3)_2$	4.01×10^{-9}
Barium iodate monohydrate	$Ba(IO_3)_2 \times H_2O$	1.67×10^{-9}
Barium molybdate	$BaMoO_4$	3.54×10^{-8}
Barium nitrate	$Ba(NO_3)_2$	4.64×10^{-3}
Barium selenate	$BaSeO_4$	3.40×10^{-8}
Barium sulfate	$BaSO_4$	1.08×10^{-10}
Barium sulfite	$BaSO_3$	5.0×10^{-10}
Beryllium hydroxide	$Be(OH)_2$	6.92×10^{-22}
Bismuth arsenate	$BiAsO_4$	4.43×10^{-10}
Bismuth iodide	BiI	7.71×10^{-19}
Cadmium arsenate	$Cd_3(AsO_4)_2$	2.2×10^{-33}
Cadmium carbonate	$CdCO_3$	1.0×10^{-12}
Cadmium fluoride	CdF_2	6.44×10^{-3}
Cadmium hydroxide	$Cd(OH)_2$	7.2×10^{-15}
Cadmium iodate	$Cd(IO_3)_2$	2.5×10^{-8}
Cadmium oxalate trihydrate	$CdC_2O_4 \times 3H_2O$	1.42×10^{-8}
Cadmium phosphate	$Cd_3(PO_4)_2$	2.53×10^{-33}
Cadmium sulfide	CdS	1×10^{-27}
Cesium perchlorate	$CsClO_4$	3.95×10^{-3}
Cesium periodate	$CsIO_4$	5.16×10^{-6}
Calcium carbonate (calcite)	$CaCO_3$	3.36×10^{-9}
Calcium carbonate (aragonite)	$CaCO_3$	6.0×10^{-9}
Calcium fluoride	CaF_2	3.45×10^{-11}
Calcium hydroxide	$Ca(OH)_2$	5.02×10^{-6}
Calcium iodate	$Ca(IO_3)_2$	6.47×10^{-6}
Calcium iodate hexahydrate	$Ca(IO_3)_2 \times 6H_2O$	7.10×10^{-7}

Calcium molybdate	CaMoO	1.46×10^{-8}
Calcium oxalate monohydrate	$CaC_2O_4\times H_2O$	2.32×10^{-9}
Calcium phosphate	$Ca_3(PO_4)_2$	2.07×10^{-33}
Calcium sulfate	$CaSO_4$	4.93×10^{-5}
Calcium sulfate dihydrate	$CaSO_4\times2H_2O$	3.14×10^{-5}
Calcium sulfate hemihydrate	$CaSO_4\times0.5H_2O$	3.1×10^{-7}
Cobalt(II) arsenate	$Co_3(AsO_4)_2$	6.80×10^{-29}
Cobalt(II) carbonate	$CoCO_3$	1.0×10^{-10}
Cobalt(II) hydroxide (blue)	$Co(OH)_2$	5.92×10^{-15}
Cobalt(II) iodate dihydrate	$Co(IO_3)_2\times2H_2O$	1.21×10^{-2}
Cobalt(II) phosphate	$Co_3(PO_4)_2$	2.05×10^{-35}
Cobalt(II) sulfide (alpha)	CoS	5×10^{-22}
Cobalt(II) sulfide (beta)	CoS	3×10^{-26}
Copper(I) bromide	CuBr	6.27×10^{-9}
Copper(I) chloride	CuCl	1.72×10^{-7}
Copper(I) cyanide	CuCN	3.47×10^{-20}
Copper(I) hydroxide *	Cu_2O	2×10^{-15}
Copper(I) iodide	CuI	1.27×10^{-12}
Copper(I) thiocyanate	CuSCN	1.77×10^{-13}
Copper(II) arsenate	$Cu_3(AsO_4)_2$	7.95×10^{-36}
Copper(II) hydroxide	$Cu(OH)_2$	4.8×10^{-20}
Copper(II) iodate monohydrate	$Cu(IO_3)_2\times H_2O$	6.94×10^{-8}
Copper(II) oxalate	CuC_2O_4	4.43×10^{-10}
Copper(II) phosphate	$Cu_3(PO_4)_2$	1.40×10^{-37}
Copper(II) sulfide	CuS	8×10^{-37}
Europium(III) hydroxide	$Eu(OH)_3$	9.38×10^{-27}
Gallium(III) hydroxide	$Ga(OH)_3$	7.28×10^{-36}
Iron(II) carbonate	$FeCO_3$	3.13×10^{-11}
Iron(II) fluoride	FeF_2	2.36×10^{-6}
Iron(II) hydroxide	$Fe(OH)_2$	4.87×10^{-17}
Iron(II) sulfide	FeS	8×10^{-19}
Iron(III) hydroxide	$Fe(OH)_3$	2.79×10^{-39}
Iron(III) phosphate dihydrate	$FePO_4\times2H_2O$	9.91×10^{-16}
Lanthanum iodate	$La(IO_3)_3$	7.50×10^{-12}
Lead(II) bromide	$PbBr_2$	6.60×10^{-6}
Lead(II) carbonate	$PbCO_3$	7.40×10^{-14}
Lead(II) chloride	$PbCl_2$	1.70×10^{-5}
Lead(II) chromate	$PbCrO_4$	3×10^{-13}

Compound	Formula	K_{sp}
Lead(II) fluoride	PbF_2	3.3×10^{-8}
Lead(II) hydroxide	$Pb(OH)_2$	1.43×10^{-20}
Lead(II) iodate	$Pb(IO_3)_2$	3.69×10^{-13}
Lead(II) iodide	PbI_2	9.8×10^{-9}
Lead(II) oxalate	PbC_2O_4	8.5×10^{-9}
Lead(II) selenate	$PbSeO_4$	1.37×10^{-7}
Lead(II) sulfate	$PbSO_4$	2.53×10^{-8}
Lead(II) sulfide	PbS	3×10^{-28}
Lithium carbonate	Li_2CO_3	8.15×10^{-4}
Lithium fluoride	LiF	1.84×10^{-3}
Lithium phosphate	Li_3PO_4	2.37×10^{-4}
Magnesium ammonium phosphate	$MgNH_4PO_4$	3×10^{-13}
Magnesium carbonate	$MgCO_3$	6.82×10^{-6}
Magnesium carbonate trihydrate	$MgCO_3 \times 3H_2O$	2.38×10^{-6}
Magnesium carbonate pentahydrate	$MgCO_3 \times 5H_2O$	3.79×10^{-6}
Magnesium fluoride	MgF_2	5.16×10^{-11}
Magnesium hydroxide	$Mg(OH)_2$	5.61×10^{-12}
Magnesium oxalate dihydrate	$MgC_2O_4 \times 2H_2O$	4.83×10^{-6}
Magnesium phosphate	$Mg_3(PO_4)_2$	1.04×10^{-24}
Manganese(II) carbonate	$MnCO_3$	2.24×10^{-11}
Manganese(II) iodate	$Mn(IO_3)_2$	4.37×10^{-7}
Manganese(II) hydroxide	$Mn(OH)_2$	2×10^{-13}
Manganese(II) oxalate dihydrate	$MnC_2O_4 \times 2H_2O$	1.70×10^{-7}
Manganese(II) sulfide (pink)	MnS	3×10^{-11}
Manganese(II) sulfide (green)	MnS	3×10^{-14}
Mercury(I) bromide	Hg_2Br_2	6.40×10^{-23}
Mercury(I) carbonate	Hg_2CO_3	3.6×10^{-17}
Mercury(I) chloride	Hg_2Cl_2	1.43×10^{-18}
Mercury(I) fluoride	Hg_2F_2	3.10×10^{-6}
Mercury(I) iodide	Hg_2I_2	5.2×10^{-29}
Mercury(I) oxalate	$Hg_2C_2O_4$	1.75×10^{-13}
Mercury(I) sulfate	Hg_2SO_4	6.5×10^{-7}
Mercury(I) thiocyanate	$Hg_2(SCN)_2$	3.2×10^{-20}
Mercury(II) bromide	$HgBr_2$	6.2×10^{-20}
Mercury(II) hydroxide	HgO	3.6×10^{-26}
Mercury(II) iodide	HgI_2	2.9×10^{-29}
Mercury(II) sulfide (black)	HgS	2×10^{-53}

Mercury(II) sulfide (red)	HgS	2×10^{-54}
Neodymium carbonate	$Nd_2(CO_3)_3$	1.08×10^{-33}
Nickel(II) carbonate	$NiCO_3$	1.42×10^{-7}
Nickel(II) hydroxide	$Ni(OH)_2$	5.48×10^{-16}
Nickel(II) iodate	$Ni(IO_3)_2$	4.71×10^{-5}
Nickel(II) phosphate	$Ni_3(PO_4)_2$	4.74×10^{-32}
Nickel(II) sulfide (alpha)	NiS	4×10^{-20}
Nickel(II) sulfide (beta)	NiS	1.3×10^{-25}
Palladium(II) thiocyanate	$Pd(SCN)_2$	4.39×10^{-23}
Potassium hexachloroplatinate	K_2PtCl_6	7.48×10^{-6}
Potassium perchlorate	$KClO_4$	1.05×10^{-2}
Potassium periodate	KIO_4	3.71×10^{-4}
Praseodymium hydroxide	$Pr(OH)_3$	3.39×10^{-24}
Radium iodate	$Ra(IO_3)_2$	1.16×10^{-9}
Radium sulfate	$RaSO_4$	3.66×10^{-11}
Rubidium perchlorate	$RuClO_4$	3.00×10^{-3}
Scandium fluoride	ScF_3	5.81×10^{-24}
Scandium hydroxide	$Sc(OH)_3$	2.22×10^{-31}
Silver(I) acetate	$AgCH_3COO$	1.94×10^{-3}
Silver(I) arsenate	Ag_3AsO_4	1.03×10^{-22}
Silver(I) bromate	$AgBrO_3$	5.38×10^{-5}
Silver(I) bromide	AgBr	5.35×10^{-13}
Silver(I) carbonate	Ag_2CO_3	8.46×10^{-12}
Silver(I) chloride	AgCl	1.77×10^{-10}
Silver(I) chromate	Ag_2CrO_4	1.12×10^{-12}
Silver(I) cyanide	AgCN	5.97×10^{-17}
Silver(I) iodate	$AgIO_3$	3.17×10^{-8}
Silver(I) iodide	AgI	8.52×10^{-17}
Silver(I) oxalate	$Ag_2C_2O_4$	5.40×10^{-12}
Silver(I) phosphate	Ag_3PO_4	8.89×10^{-17}
Silver(I) sulfate	Ag_2SO_4	1.20×10^{-5}
Silver(I) sulfite	Ag_2SO_3	1.50×10^{-14}
Silver(I) sulfide	Ag_2S	8×10^{-51}
Silver(I) thiocyanate	AgSCN	1.03×10^{-12}
Strontium arsenate	$Sr_3(AsO_4)_2$	4.29×10^{-19}
Strontium carbonate	$SrCO_3$	5.60×10^{-10}
Strontium fluoride	SrF_2	4.33×10^{-9}
Strontium iodate	$Sr(IO_3)_2$	1.14×10^{-7}

Name	Formula	K_{sp}
Strontium iodate monohydrate	$Sr(IO_3)_2 \times H_2O$	3.77×10^{-7}
Strontium iodate hexahydrate	$Sr(IO_3)_2 \times 6H_2O$	4.55×10^{-7}
Strontium oxalate	SrC_2O_4	5×10^{-8}
Strontium sulfate	$SrSO_4$	3.44×10^{-7}
Thallium(I) bromate	$TlBrO_3$	1.10×10^{-4}
Thallium(I) bromide	$TlBr$	3.71×10^{-6}
Thallium(I) chloride	$TlCl$	1.86×10^{-4}
Thallium(I) chromate	Tl_2CrO_4	8.67×10^{-13}
Thallium(I) hydroxide	$Tl(OH)_3$	1.68×10^{-44}
Thallium(I) iodate	$TlIO_3$	3.12×10^{-6}
Thallium(I) iodide	TlI	5.54×10^{-8}
Thallium(I) thiocyanate	$TlSCN$	1.57×10^{-4}
Thallium(I) sulfide	Tl_2S	6×10^{-22}
Tin(II) hydroxide	$Sn(OH)_2$	5.45×10^{-27}
Yttrium carbonate	$Y_2(CO_3)_3$	1.03×10^{-31}
Yttrium fluoride	YF_3	8.62×10^{-21}
Yttrium hydroxide	$Y(OH)_3$	1.00×10^{-22}
Yttrium iodate	$Y(IO_3)_3$	1.12×10^{-10}
Zinc arsenate	$Zn_3(AsO_4)_2$	2.8×10^{-28}
Zinc carbonate	$ZnCO_3$	1.46×10^{-10}
Zinc carbonate monohydrate	$ZnCO_3 \times H_2O$	5.42×10^{-11}
Zinc fluoride	ZnF	3.04×10^{-2}
Zinc hydroxide	$Zn(OH)_2$	3×10^{-17}
Zinc iodate dihydrate	$Zn(IO_3)_2 \times 2H_2O$	4.1×10^{-6}
Zinc oxalate dihydrate	$ZnC_2O_4 \times 2H_2O$	1.38×10^{-9}
Zinc selenide	$ZnSe$	3.6×10^{-26}
Zinc selenite monohydrate	$ZnSe \times H_2O$	1.59×10^{-7}
Zinc sulfide (alpha)	ZnS	2×10^{-25}
Zinc sulfide (beta)	ZnS	3×10^{-23}

(*) $Cu_2O + H_2O \rightleftharpoons 2 Cu^+ + 2 OH^-$
(**) $HgO + H_2O \rightleftharpoons Hg^{2+} + 2 OH^-$

Factorial Design

Two-level 2-Factor Full-Factorial Experiment Design Pattern

RUN	Combination	Factors	
		A	B
1	(1)	-	-
2	a	+	-
3	b	-	+
$4 = 2^2$	ab	+	+

Two-level 3-Factor Full-Factorial Experiment Design Pattern

RUN	Combination	Factors		
		A	B	C
1	(1)	-	-	-
2	a	+	-	-
3	b	-	+	-
4	ab	+	+	-
5	c	-	-	+
6	ac	+	-	+
7	bc	-	+	+
$8 = 2^3$	abc	+	+	+

Two-level 4-Factor Full-Factorial Experiment Design Pattern

RUN	Comb.	Factors			
		A	B	C	D
1	(1)	-	-	-	-
2	a	+	-	-	-
3	b	-	+	-	-
4	ab	+	+	-	-
5	c	-	-	+	-
6	ac	+	-	+	-
7	bc	-	+	+	-
8	abc	+	+	+	-
9	d	-	-	-	+
10	ad	+	-	-	+
11	bd	-	+	-	+
12	abd	+	+	-	+
13	cd	-	-	+	+
14	acd	+	-	+	+
15	bcd	-	+	+	+
$16 = 2^4$	abcd	+	+	+	+

Two-level 5-Factor Full-Factorial Experiment Design Pattern

RUN	Comb.	Factors				
		A	B	C	D	E
1	(1)	-	-	-	-	-
2	a	+	-	-	-	-
3	b	-	+	-	-	-
4	ab	+	+	-	-	-
5	c	-	-	+	-	-
6	ac	+	-	+	-	-
7	bc	-	+	+	-	-
8	abc	+	+	+	-	-
RUN	Comb.	A	B	C	D	E
9	d	-	-	-	+	-
10	ad	+	-	-	+	-
11	bd	-	+	-	+	-
12	abd	+	+	-	+	-
13	cd	-	-	+	+	-
14	acd	+	-	+	+	-
15	bcd	-	+	+	+	-
16	abcd	+	+	+	+	-
17	e	-	-	-	-	+
18	ae	+	-	-	-	+
19	be	-	+	-	-	+
20	abe	+	+	-	-	+
21	ce	-	-	+	-	+
22	ace	+	-	+	-	+
23	bce	-	+	+	-	+
24	abce	+	+	+	-	+
25	de	-	-	-	+	+
26	ade	+	-	-	+	+
27	bde	-	+	-	+	+
28	abde	+	+	-	+	+
29	cde	-	-	+	+	+
30	acde	+	-	+	+	+
31	bcde	-	+	+	+	+
$32 = 2^5$	abcde	+	+	+	+	+

2-Factor Full-Factorial Experiment Design Computing Table

RUN	Comb.	I	A	B	AB
1	(1)	+	-	-	+
2	a	+	+	-	-
3	b	+	-	+	-
$4 = 2^2$	ab	+	+	+	+

3-Factor Full-Factorial Experiment Design Computing Table

RUN	Comb.	I	A	B	AB	C	AC	BC	ABC
1	(1)	+	-	-	+	-	+	+	-
2	a	+	+	-	-	-	-	+	+
3	b	+	-	+	-	-	+	-	+
4	ab	+	+	+	+	-	-	-	-
5	c	+	-	-	+	+	-	-	+
6	ac	+	+	-	-	+	+	-	-
7	bc	+	-	+	-	+	-	+	-
$8 = 2^3$	abc	+	+	+	+	+	+	+	+

Properties table of common solvents

The solvents are grouped into non-polar, polar aprotic and polar protic solvents and ordered by increasing polarity. The polarity is given as the dielectric constant. The density of nonpolar solvents that are heavier than water is bolded.

Solvent	Chemical Formula	Boiling point	Dielectric constant	Density
Non-Polar Solvents				
Hexane	$CH_3-CH_2-CH_2-CH_2-CH_2-CH_3$	69 °C	2.0	0.655 g/ml
Benzene	C_6H_6	80 °C	2.3	0.879 g/ml
Toluene	$C_6H_5-CH_3$	111 °C	2.4	0.867 g/ml
Diethyl ether	$CH_3CH_2-O-CH_2-CH_3$	35 °C	4.3	0.713 g/ml
Chloroform	$CHCl_3$	61 °C	4.8	**1.498 g/ml**
Ethyl acetate	$CH_3-C(=O)-O-CH_2-CH_3$	77 °C	6.0	0.894 g/ml
Dichloromethane	CH_2Cl_2	40 °C	9.1	**1.326 g/ml**
Polar Aprotic Solvents				
1,4-Dioxane	$/-CH_2-CH_2-O-CH_2-CH_2-O-\backslash$	101 °C	2.3	1.033 g/ml
Tetrahydrofuran (THF)	$/-CH_2-CH_2-O-CH_2-CH_2-\backslash$	66 °C	7.5	0.886 g/ml
Acetone	$CH_3-C(=O)-CH_3$	56 °C	21	0.786 g/ml
Acetonitrile (MeCN)	$CH_3-C\equiv N$	82 °C	37	0.786 g/ml
Dimethylformamide (DMF)	$H-C(=O)N(CH_3)_2$	153 °C	38	0.944 g/ml

Dimethyl sulfoxide (DMSO)	CH_3-S(=O)-CH_3	189 °C	47	**1.092 g/ml**
Polar Protic Solvents				
Acetic acid	CH_3-C(=O)OH	118 °C	6.2	**1.049 g/ml**
n-Butanol	CH_3-CH_2-CH_2-CH_2-OH	118 °C	18	0.810 g/ml
Isopropanol	CH_3-CH(-OH)-CH_3	82 °C	18	0.785 g/ml
n-Propanol	CH_3-CH_2-CH_2-OH	97 °C	20	0.803 g/ml
Ethanol	CH_3-CH_2-OH	79 °C	24	0.789 g/ml
Methanol	CH_3-OH	65 °C	33	0.791 g/ml
Formic acid	H-C(=O)OH	100 °C	58	**1.21 g/ml**
Water	H-O-H	100 °C	80	1.000 g/ml

Ester Name	Molar Mass (g/mol)	Structure	Odor or Occurrence
Allyl hexanoate			pineapple
Benzyl acetate	150.18		pear, strawberry, jasmine
Bornyl acetate			pine tree flavor
Butyl butyrate	144.21		pineapple
Ethyl acetate	88.12		nail polish remover, model paint, model airplane glue
Ethyl butyrate	116.16		banana, pineapple, strawberry
Ethyl hexanoate			strawberry
Ethyl cinnamate	176.21		cinnamon
Ethyl formate	74.08		lemon, rum, strawberry
Ethyl heptanoate	158.27		apricot, cherry, grape, raspberry
Ethyl isovalerate			apple
Ethyl lactate	118.13		butter cream
Ethyl nonanoate			grape
Ethyl valerate	130.18		apple
Geranyl acetate	196.29		geranium
Geranyl butyrate			cherry
Geranyl pentanoate			apple
Isobutyl acetate	116.16		cherry, raspberry, strawberry
Isobutyl formate			raspberries
Isoamyl acetate	130.19		pear, banana (flavoring in Pear Drops)
Isopropyl acetate	102.1		fruity
Linalyl acetate			lavender, sage
Linalyl butyrate			peach
Linalyl formate			apple, peach

Name	MW	Structure	Aroma
Methyl acetate	74.08		peppermint
Methyl anthranilate	151.165		grape, jasmine
Methyl benzoate	136.15		fruity, ylang ylang, feijoa fruit
Methyl benzyl acetate			cherry
Methyl butyrate	102.13		pineapple, apple
Methyl cinnamate			strawberry
Methyl pentanoate	116.16		flowery
Methyl phenyl acetate			honey
Methyl salicylate (oil of wintergreen)	152.1494		root beer, wintergreen
Nonyl caprylate			orange
Octyl acetate	172.27		fruity-orange
Octyl butyrate			parsnip
Amyl acetate (pentyl acetate)	130.19		apple, banana
Pentyl butyrate (amyl butyrate)	158.24		apricot, pear, pineapple
Pentyl hexanoate (amyl caproate)			apple, pineapple
Pentyl pentanoate (amyl valerate)	172.15		apple
Propyl ethanoate			pear
Propyl isobutyrate			rum
Terpenyl butyrate			cherry

Glycol Ethers

Chemical Name	Molecular wt	Flash Point °F	Surface tension (dynes/cm)	Solubility in water (ml/100ml)
Propylene Glycol Methyl Ether	90.1	90[1]	22.7	∞
Dipropylene Glycol Methyl Ether	148.2	167[1]	28.8	∞
Tripropylene Glycol Methyl Ether	206.3	232[1]	30.0	∞
Propylene Glycol n-Butyl Ether	132.2	138[2]	26.3	7.3
Dipropylene Glycol n-Butyl Ether	190.3	212[1]	28.8	5.5
Ethylene Glycol n-Butyl Ether	118.2	150[2]	27.4	∞
Diethylene Glycol Methyl Ether	120.1	197[1]	34.8	∞

	viscosity [Pa·s]	viscosity [cP]
acetone	[a] 0.306×10^{-3}	[a] 0.306
methanol	[a] 0.544×10^{-3}	[a] 0.544
benzene	[a] 0.604×10^{-3}	[a] 0.604
ethanol	[a] 1.074×10^{-3}	[a] 1.074
mercury	[a] 1.526×10^{-3}	[a] 1.526
nitrobenzene	[a] 1.863×10^{-3}	[a] 1.863
propanol	[a] 1.945×10^{-3}	[a] 1.945
sulfuric acid	[a] 24.2×10^{-3}	[a] 24.2
olive oil	81×10^{-3}	81
glycerol	[a] 934×10^{-3}	[a] 934
castor oil	985×10^{-3}	985
HFO-380	2022×10^{-3}	2022
pitch	2.3×10^8	230

	viscosity [cP]
honey	2,000–10,000
molasses	5,000–10,000
molten glass	10,000–1,000,000
chocolate syrup	10,000–25,000
chocolate*	45,000–130,000 [2]
ketchup*	50,000–100,000
peanut butter	~250,000
shortening*	~250,000

* These materials are highly non-Newtonian

Indicator	pH Range	Quantity per 10 ml	Acid	Base
Thymol Blue	1.2-2.8	1-2 drops 0.1% soln. in aq.	red	yellow
Pentamethoxy red	1.2-2.3	1 drop 0.1% soln. in 70% alc.	red-violet	colorless
Tropeolin OO	1.3-3.2	1 drop 1% aq. soln.	red	yellow
2,4-Dinitrophenol	2.4-4.0	1-2 drops 0.1% soln. in 50% alc.	colorless	yellow
Methyl yellow	2.9-4.0	1 drop 0.1% soln. in 90% alc.	red	yellow
Methyl orange	3.1-4.4	1 drop 0.1% aq. soln.	red	orange
Bromphenol blue	3.0-4.6	1 drop 0.1% aq. soln.	yellow	blue-violet
Tetrabromphenol blue	3.0-4.6	1 drop 0.1% aq. soln.	yellow	blue
Alizarin sodium sulfonate	3.7-5.2	1 drop 0.1% aq. soln.	yellow	violet
□-Naphthyl red	3.7-5.0	1 drop 0.1% soln. in 70% alc.	red	yellow
p-Ethoxychrysoidine	3.5-5.5	1 drop 0.1% aq. soln.	red	yellow
Bromcresol green	4.0-5.6	1 drop 0.1% aq. soln.	yellow	blue
Methyl red	4.4-6.2	1 drop 0.1% aq. soln.	red	yellow
Bromcresol purple	5.2-6.8	1 drop 0.1% aq. soln.	yellow	purple
Chlorphenol red	5.4-6.8	1 drop 0.1% aq. soln.	yellow	red
Bromphenol blue	6.2-7.6	1 drop 0.1% aq. soln.	yellow	blue
p-Nitrophenol	5.0-7.0	1-5 drops 0.1% aq. soln.	colorless	yellow
Azolitmin	5.0-8.0	5 drops 0.5% aq. soln.	red	blue
Phenol red	6.4-8.0	1 drop 0.1% aq. soln.	yellow	red
Neutral red	6.8-8.0	1 drop 0.1% soln. in 70% alc.	red	yellow
Rosolic acid	6.8-8.0	1 drop 0.1% soln. in 90% alc.	yellow	red
Cresol red	7.2-8.8	1 drop 0.1% aq. soln.	yellow	red
□-Naphtholphthalein	7.3-8.7	1-5 drops 0.1% soln. in 70% alc.	rose	green
Tropeolin OOO	7.6-8.9	1 drop 0.1% aq. soln.	yellow	rose-red
Thymol blue	8.0-9.6	1-5 drops 0.1% aq. soln.	yellow	blue
Phenolphthalein	8.0-10.0	1-5 drops 0.1% soln. in 70% alc.	colorless	red
□-Naphtholbenzein	9.0-11.0	1-5 drops 0.1% soln. in 90% alc.	yellow	blue
Thymolphthalein	9.4-10.6	1 drop 0.1% soln. in 90% alc.	colorless	blue
Nile blue	10.1-11.1	1 drop 0.1% aq. soln.	blue	red
Alizarin yellow	10.0-12.0	1 drop 0.1% aq. soln.	yellow	lilac
Salicyl yellow	10.0-12.0	1-5 drops 0.1% soln. in 90% alc.	yellow	orange-brown
Diazo violet	10.1-12.0	1 drop 0.1% aq. soln.	yellow	violet
Tropeolin O	11.0-13.0	1 drop 0.1% aq. soln.	yellow	orange-brown

Nitramine	11.0-13.0	1-2 drops 0.1% soln in 70% alc.	colorless	orange-brown
Poirrier's blue	11.0-13.0	1 drop 0.1% aq. soln.	blue	violet-pink
Trinitrobenzoic acid	12.0-13.4	1 drop 0.1% aq. soln.	colorless	orange-red

SI Unit Prefixes

Factors	Prefix	Symbol
10^{12}	tera	T
19^9	giga	G
10^6	mega	M
10^3	kilo	k
10^2	hecto	h
10^1	deca	da
10^{-1}	deci	d
10^{-2}	centi	c
10^{-3}	milli	m
10^{-6}	micro	μ
10^{-9}	nano	n
10^{-12}	pico	p
10^{-15}	femto	f
10^{-18}	atto	a

Useful Constants

Acceleration of Gravity	9.806 m/s^2
Avogadro's Number	6.022×10^{23}
Electronic Charge	1.602×10^{-19} C
Faraday Constant	9.6485×10^4 J/V
Gas Constant	0.08206 L·atm/(mol·K) 8.314 J/(mol·K) 8.314×10^7 g·cm^2/(s^2·mol·K)
Planck's Constant	6.626×10^{-34} J·s
Speed of Light	2.998×10^8 m/s
π	3.14159
e	2.718
$\ln x$	$2.3026 \log x$
2.3026 R	19.14 J/(mol·K)
2.3026 RT (at 25°C)	5.708 kJ/mol

Quantity	SI Unit	Other Unit	Conversion Factor
Energy	joule	calorie erg	1 cal = 4.184 J 1 erg = 10^{-7} J
Force	newton	dyne	1 dyn = 10^{-5} N
Length	metre	ångström	1 Å = 10^{-10} m = 10^{-8} cm = 10^{-1} nm
Mass	kilogram	pound	1 lb = 0.453592 kg
Pressure	pascal	bar atmosphere mm Hg lb/in^2	1 bar = 10^5 Pa 1 atm = 1.01325×10^5 Pa 1 mm Hg = 133.322 Pa 1 lb/in^2 = 6894.8 Pa
Temperature	kelvin	Celsius Fahrenheit	1°C = 1 K 1°F = 5/9 K
Volume	cubic metre	litre gallon (U.S.) gallon (U.K.) cubic inch	1 L = 1 dm^3 = 10^{-3} m^3 1 gal (U.S.) = 3.7854×10^{-3} m^3 1 gal (U.K.) = 4.5641×10^{-3} m^3 1 in^3 = 1.6387×10^{-6} m^3

Common Qualitative Analysis Reagents

Reagent	Effects
6M HCl	Increases $[H^+]$ Increases $[Cl^-]$ Decreases $[OH^-]$ Dissolves insoluble carbonates, chromates, hydroxides, some sulfates Destroys hydroxo and NH_3 complexes Precipitates insoluble chlorides
6M HNO_3	Increases $[H^+]$ Decreases $[OH^-]$ Dissolves insoluble carbonates, chromates, and hydroxides Dissolves insoluble sulfides by oxidizing sulfide ion Destroys hydroxo and ammonia complexes Good oxidizing agent when hot
6 M NaOH	Increases $[OH^-]$ Decreases $[H^+]$ Forms hydroxo complexes Precipitates insoluble hydroxides
6M NH_3	Increases $[NH_3]$ Increases $[OH^-]$ Decreases $[H^+]$ Precipitates insoluble hydroxides Forms NH_3 complexes Forms a basic buffer with NH_4^+

Complexes of Cations with NH_3 and OH^-

Cation	NH_3 Complex	OH^- Complex
Ag^+	$Ag(NH_3)_2^+$	--
Al^{3+}	--	$Al(OH)_4^-$
Cd^{2+}	$Cd(NH_3)_4^{2+}$	--
Cu^{2+}	$Cu(NH_3)_4^{2+}$ (blue)	--
Ni^{2+}	$Ni(NH_3)_6^{2+}$ (blue)	--
Pb^{2+}	--	$Pb(OH)_3^-$
Sb^{3+}	--	$Sb(OH)_4^-$
Sn^{4+}	--	$Sn(OH)_6^{2-}$
Zn^{2+}	$Zn(NH_3)_4^{2+}$	$Zn(OH)_4^{2-}$

Incompatible Chemical Mixtures

Acids with cyanide salts or cyanide solution. Generates highly toxic hydrogen cyanide gas.

Acids with sulfide salts or sulfide solutions. Generates highly toxic hydrogen sulfide gas.

Acids with bleach. Generates highly toxic chlorine gas.

Oxidizing acids (e.g., nitric acid, perchloric acid) with combustible materials (e.g., paper, alcohols, and other common solvents). May result in fire.

Solid oxidizers (e.g., permanganates, iodates, nitrates) with combustible materials (e.g., paper, alcohols, other common solvents).

May result in fire.

Hydrides (e.g., sodium hydride) with water. May form flammable hydrogen gas.

Phosphides (e.g., sodium phosphide) with water. May form highly toxic phosphine gas.

Silver salts with ammonia in the presence of a strong base. May generate an explosively unstable solid.

Alkali metals (e.g., sodium, potassium) with water. May form flammable hydrogen gas.

Oxidizing agents (e.g., nitric acid) with reducing agents (e.g., hydrazine). May cause fires or explosions.

Unsaturated compounds (e.g., substances containing carbonyls or double bonds) in the presence of acids or bases. May polymerize violently.

Hydrogen peroxide/acetone mixtures when heated in the presence of an acid. May cause explosions.

Hydrogen peroxide/acetic acid mixtures. May explode upon heating.

Hydrogen peroxide/sulfuric acid mixtures. May spontaneously detonate.

References

1. *CRC Handbook of Chemistry and Physics*, Ed. D. R. Lide, The Chemical Rubber Co., 1999.

2. Guide for the Use of the International System of Units, *National Institute of Standards and Technology Special Publication 811*, B. N. Taylor, Washington, 1995

3. IUPAC definition of the Poise
 Massey, B. S. (1983). Mechanics of Fluids, fifth ed. ISBN 0-442-30552-4.

4. Symon, Keith (1971). Mechanics. Addison-Wesley, Reading, MA. ISBN 0-201-07392-7.

5. Landau, L. D.; Lifshitz, E. M. (1997). Fluid Mechanics (Course of Theoretical Physics Volume 6), (Translated from Russian by J.B. Sykes and W.H. Reid), Second ed., Boston, MA: Butterworth Heinemann. ISBN 0-7506-2767-0.

6. Serway, Raymond A (1996), Physics For Scientist & Engineers (4th Edition 2nd Printing ed.), Saunders College Publishing

7. International Standard ISO 31-8: Quantities and units – Part 8: Physical chemistry and molecular physics, Annex C (normative): pH. International Organization for Standardization, 1992.

8. Definitions of pH scales, standard reference values, measurement of pH, and related terminology. Pure Appl. Chem. (1985), 57, pp 531–542.

9. White, Harvey E. Modern College Physics, van Nostrand 1948

10. John W. M. Bush (May 2004). MIT Lecture Notes on Surface Tension, lecture 5. Massachusetts Institute of Technology. Retrieved on April 1, 2007.

11. John W. M. Bush (April 2004). MIT Lecture Notes on Surface Tension, lecture 1. Massachusetts Institute of Technology. Retrieved on April 1, 2007.

12. John W. M. Bush (May 2004). MIT Lecture Notes on Surface Tension, lecture 3. Massachusetts Institute of Technology. Retrieved on April 1, 2007.

13. Sears, Francis Weston; Zemanski, Mark W. University Physics 2nd ed. Addison Wesley 1955

14. Aaronson, Scott, "NP-Complete Problems and physical reality." SIGACT News

15. Lamb, Sir Horace Hydrodynamics, 6th ed. Dover 1932

16. G. Ertl, H. Knözinger and J. Weitkamp; Handbook of heterogeneous catalysis, Vol. 2, page 430; Wiley-VCH; Weinheim; 1997

17. GC/MS Eiceman, G.A. (2000). Gas Chromatography. In R.A. Meyers (Ed.), Encyclopedia of Analytical Chemistry: Applications, Theory, and Instrumentation, pp. 10627. Chichester: Wiley. ISBN 0-471-97670-9

18. Gas Chromatography. In Scientific Evidence 2, pp. 362. Charlottesville: Lexis Law Publishing. ISBN 0-327-04985-5.

19. S. B. Smith, Jr and G. M. Hieftje, Appl. Spectrosc., 1983, 37, 419–424

20. Hplc 2007 Waters Corporation

21. Sulfuric Greenwood, N.N. and A. Earnshaw. Chemistry of the Elements, pp 837-845. Pergamon Press, Oxford, UK, 1984.

22. Phosphoric acid. The Columbia Encyclopedia, Sixth Edition. 2001-05

23. A Dictionary of Science, Oxford University Press Inc., New York 2003 Excerpts from US Federal Register: June 2, 1998
(Volume 63, Number 105)]

24. (Design of Experiments Frank Yates and Kenneth Mather (1963).

25. Post Mixing Optimization and Solutions Copyright © 2003, 2004,2005,2006,2007

26. SiliconFarEast.com, Copyright © 2005

INDEX

A

140 Solvent(Aliphatic solvent)
138
9% Manganese NuXtra drier
162
9% Manganese NuXtra drier
163
Acetic acid
33, 36, 59, 201
Acid-base
105
acidity
8, 9, 28, 31, 33, 35, 51, 98
acids
21, 22, 24, 27, 28, 31- 34,37,39, 40, 41, 54,
57, 75, 76, 80, 86, 88,97, 103, 104, 105, 109,
201,
Adipic acid
34
Adjustable cell constant
102
Adjustable temperature coefficients
102
Alcohol
15, 19, 41, 42, 53, 54, 57, 59, 61, 62, 65,
94, 97, 102, 121, 123, 134, 140, 145, 153,
156, 167, 201
Alfonic 1012-40 additive (Ethoxylate) 125

Aliphatic
54, 62, 87, 89, 138
alkalinity
8, 87, 98
Alkanolamide: Coconut (fatty acid)
85
Alkanolamides
84
Alkylether Hydroxypropyl Sultaine
76
Alox 2028
138
Amines
54, 62, 69
Ammonia
9, 38, 39, 44, 49, 51, 53, 54, 62, 106, 111,
201
Ammonium bifluoride
137
Ammonium chloride
43, 44, 45, 49,

Ammonium dihydrogen phosphate
51

Ammonium hydroxide
146,147,161
Ammonium Laureth Sulfate
78, 79
Ammonium Linear Alcohol ether Sulfate
79
Ammonium nitrate
49
Ammonium Nonylphenol Ether Sulfate
79
Ammonium phosphate
51
Ammonium sulfate
53

Amphoteric
65, 74, 75, 90, 92, 125, 145, 158
Amyl Acetate
170
ANALYSIS METHODS
97
Anion exchange
109

Anionic
64, 74, 75, 78, 80, 81, 89, 90
aprotic solvents
18, 192
Aromatic
54, 55, 56, 62, 69, 87, 88, 89
Atomic absorption spectroscopy
107
AUTOMOTIVE CARE PRODUCTS
164
Autoranging
102

B

Baffles
118, 119, 120
bases
21, 24, 32, 38, 40, 60, 62, 75, 76, 80, 88, 114,
201

204

basic
8, 9, 10, 11, 26, 28, 47, 50, 56, 69, 72, 74, 98, 99, 100,105, 106
Bezyl Trimonium Chloride
82
Bioaffinity chromatography
115
Block Polymers
88
Blocking
93
BOILING POINT
6, 11, 12, 23, 25, 36, 54, 59, 62
Borax
43
Bubble pressure method
16

C

Cabosil M-5
131
Calcium
17, 26, 28, 30, 35, 36, 42, 44, 45, 46, 48, 52, 53, 79, 81, 91, 92, 105
Calcium chloride
30, 42, 44, 45, 46
Capillary rise method
16
carbonate
17, 26, 28, 30, 38, 41, 42, 43, 125, 126, 149, 158
Carbopol 941
164
Cation exchange
109
Cationic
64, 74, 75, 77, 80, 82, 90, 133
centipoise
7
Cetyl Trimonium Bromide
82
Chelating agents
91, 92
chelator
21, 92
Chelon 10 (EDTA)
126, 127
Chelon 100
127, 150, 151, 152, 153, 155, 157, 158, 164, 168,169,170
Chelon 120
153
Chemical Compatibility
116

CHEMICAL MIXING/BLENDING
116
Chloride
17, 27, 28, 44, 46, 58
Citric acid
21, 30, 32, 33, 34, 35, 37, 148, 153
Cleaning
65
closed cup
11
Cocamidopropyl Betaine
76
Cocamidopropyl Hydroxy Sultaine
77
Cocamine Oxide
82
Coco/Oleamidopropyl Betaine
76
Cocoamidopropyl Betaine
165
Coconut Hydroxyethyl Imidazoline
83

Colloid 646
136
Colloidal Silica
146, 147
Comparison
93

Complex Ditallow Sulfate Quaternary
82
Complex metric titration
105
Conductivity
23, 99, 100, 101, 102, 110
Control variable
93
Controlled Dissolution
71
copper(II) sulfate
24, 52
Cyclohexylamine
142

D

DENSITY
6, 16, 19, 25, 38, 59, 80, 97, 115

Desolvation
107
Dial Reading Viscometer
98

Diammonium hydrogen phosphate
51
Diethanolamide: Coco/Lauric (fatty acid)
84
Diethanolamide: Coconut (fatty acid)
84
Diethanolamide: Lauric (fatty acid)
84
Diethanolamide: Linoleic (fatty acid)
84
Diethanolamine
142

Diethylene Glycol Monostearate
85
Dihydroxyethyl Tallow Glycinate
77
Dinonylphenol Aromatic Ethoxylates
87
Disodium Capryloampho Diacetate
75, 138
Disodium Capryloampho Dipropionate
76
Disodium Cocoampho Dipropionate
76
Disodium Dodecyl Diphenyl Oxide
Disulfonate
80
Disodium Lauramide (MEA)
Sulfosuccinate
80
Disodium Laureth (3) Sulfosuccinate
80
Disodium Lauroampho Diacetate
75

Disodium Lauryl Sulfosuccinate
80
Disodium N-Alkyl Sulfosuccinamate
81
Disodium Ricinoleamide (MEA)
 Sulfosuccinate
80
Dispersions
66
d-Limonene
130, 131, 156, 164
Dodecylbenzene Sulfonic Acid
126, 152, 157, 166

Dodecylphenol Aromatic Ethoxylates
87
Dowfax 2A1
136, 143, 144, 147, 154
DOWICIDE 1
144, 151, 152, 162, 163, 164, 166

DOWICIDE A1 antimicrobial
143
Drop volume method
16
Du Noüy Ring method
 15
Duponol C
146
DV-E Viscometer
98
Dye
129, 133, 134, 137, 145, 146,
148-153, 157, 158, 165
Dye (acid/water soluble)
128
Dye (Yellow color)
150
Dye (Color)
126
Dye (orange color)
131
Dye (water soluble)
134

E

Electrostatic Stabilization
67

EMULSIFICATION
 65, 66, 72, 74, 86
Emulsifier 4
165
emulsion
19, 20 36, 53, 69, 72, 73, 74, 78,
79, 81, 83, 85, 87, 118, 164, 166
ESI-CYRL 4100
 162, 163
ESI-CYRL 645
162, 163

Esters
36, 40, 57, 59, 85, 86, 89
ethanol
18, 19, 34, 57, 59, 111, 125
Ethoxylated Alkanolamide: Coconut
(fatty acid)
 85
Ethoxylated Mercaptans
88
Ethoxylated Oils: Caster Oil
86
Ethylene Glycol
131

Ethylene Glycol Distearate
85
Ethylene Glycol Monostearate
85
Exkin#2(antiskinning agent)
162, 163

EXPERIMENT/TESTING METHOD
93

F

Factorial experiment
94
Ferric chloride
47
FLASH POINT
6, 11, 55, 56
Flocculent
131
Fluent Lub or Ucon Fluid Lub
140
Fluoride
31, 48, 49

Foaming
67, 68, 74, 75, 76, 77, 78, 79,
80, 81, 87, 89, 132, 145, 166
freezing point
6
FTIR (Fourier Transform Infrared)
Spectroscopy
110

G

Gas chromatography-mass spectrometry
108

Gel Formation
68
Germaben II
131
Germaben II-E
133
Gibbs free energy
13, 14
Gluconic acid
35

hydrochloric acid

Glycerin
143, 144
Glycerol Monostearate
85
Glycol Ether DPM
124, 126, 135, 141, 143, 144, 146,
147, 155, 159, 168, 170
Glycol Ether DPnB
123, 126, 146
Glycol Ether EB
127, 129, 136, 137, 145, 148, 152, 157,
165, 167
Glycol Ether PM
124, 141, 145, 146, 147, 154, 160, 161,
169, 170
Glycol Ether PnB
121, 122, 123, 124, 125, 126, 127, 146, 154,
155, 161, 169
Glycol Ether TPM
124
Glycol ethers
61, 122-170
Glycol ethers esters
59
Glycolic acid
35, 36
Glycols
54, 59, 60, 61, 62, 85, 86, 88,
89, 90, 121, 122, 123-127, 129,
131, 135, 137, 141, 143-150,154,
155, 157, 159, 160,161,-170
Glydant (antimicrobial)
127

Glydant (Dimethyl hydantoin)
127

H

Halogenated solvents
54, 58
Henderson-Hasselbalch equation
104
High-performance liquid
chromatography
112
HLB
66, 72, 73
homogeneous
6, 18, 21
Hostacar BS (corrosion inhibitor)
140
HOUSEHOLD CLEANING PRODUCTS
143
KEROSENE

9, 22, 27, 28, 29, 30, 36, 39, 44, 77, 83, 128, 148
Hydrofluoric acid
30, 31, 48, 138
hydrometer
6, 97
hydrophilic
18, 64, 67, 69, 70, 72, 78, 82, 84, 113
hydroxyacetic acid
35, 145,
Hydroxypropyl methylcellulose
129

I

Igepal CO-530
168
Igepal Co-630
122, 135,159, 170
Independent variable
94
INDUSTRIAL AND HOUSEHOLD BASE PRODUCT FORMULATIONS
121

INDUSTRIAL CLEANER PRODUCTS
121
Ion-exchange chromatography
109, 115
Isopar-m
164
Isopropanol
146, 159, 170
Isopropyl Alcohol
134, 145,153, 156, 167
Isopropylamine Dodecylbenzene Sulfonate
79

J

Jean Louis Marie Poiseuille
7

K

Kaopolite 1152
165
Kelzan S
136,145, 148

141

kinematic viscosities
7, 8

L

Laponite RDS
136
Lard Oil #2
139
Larostat 264A
156
Lauramidopropyl Betaine
76
Lauramine Oxide
82, 132
Lemon Scent
150
Linear Alcohol Ethoxylates
87

Linear Calcium Dodecylbenzene Sulfonate
79
lipophilic
18, 72, 85, 86
Lubrican
7, 34, 69, 82, 84, 85, 86, 127, 140, 166, 169

M

Magnesium Lauryl Sulfate
78
Malic Acid
148
Maquat (Quaternary ammonium)
149
mass
6, 13, 108, 109, 119
Methanol
129, 167
Methylene Chloride
129
Mineral Seal Oil
165
Mineral Spirits
125, 130, 131, 162, 163

Miramine OC surfactant
124
Miranol C2M
141
Miranol C2M-Sf Amphoteric
125
Miranol CM emulsifier
169
miscibility
6, 18, 19
mixture
11, 17, 18, 19, 21, 32, 43, 53, 56, 58, 61, 68, 69, 71, 73, 81, 97, 103, 107, 108, 111- 114, 118, 201
molarity
8, 9, 28,
Monafax 1293
164
Monateric CA-35
145
Monochlorotoluene
167

Mono-Ethanolamide: Coconut
84
Monoethanolamine (MEA)
125, 144
Mono-Isopropanolamide
85, 168
Monoprotic
26, 27, 28, 104, 105
Morpholine
164

Myrtrimonium Bromide
82

N

N-Butanol
162, 163
Neodol 1-3
156
Neodol 1-7
153, 156
Neodol 25-3 Linear Alcohol Ethoxylate
121
Neodol 25-7 Linear Alcohol Ethoxylate
121
Neodol 91-6 Linear Alcohol Ethoxylate
123
neutral
8, 10, 52, 98, 99, 126, 127,
neutralization
29, 39, 40, 105

Newton
7, 13, 118
Niaproof 08
161
Ninol 11 CM
130, 134, 169
Ninol 1281
169
Ninol 1285 Alkylolamide
155
Ninol 1285 Alkylolamide
124

Nitrate
17, 25, 26, 49, 50
nitric acid
22, 25, 26, 27, 50, 57, 201
Nocco 100 oil #100-S
139
Nonionic
64, 67, 68, 72, 73, 74, 75, 79, 84, 85, 86, 87, 89, 90, 122, 145, 167
Nonionic Esters: Glycerol
85
Nonionic Esters: Glycols
85
Nonionic Ethoxylated Oils
86
Nonionic Ethoxylates
87
Nonionic Polyethylene Glycol Esters
85
Nonionic Sorbitol and
Ethoxylated Sorbitol Esters
86
Nonylphenol Aromatic Ethoxylates
87
Normal phase
113

O

Octylphenol Aromatic Ethoxylates
87
o-dichlorobenzene
135
Odorless Mineral Spirits
157
Oleamidopropyl Betaine
76
Oleic Acid
123, 143, 144, 159, 160, 164
Oleyl Alcohol Ethoxylates
88

Oleyl Hydroxyethyl Imidazoline
83
open cup
11
Order of Addition
118
Organic acid
33, 34, 36, 37, 48

Orthogonality
93
Orvus K
154

Oxalic acid
33, 36, 104

P

Paraffin Wax
129
Pendant drop method
16
Pensky-Martens
11
Perchloroethylene
159, 168
Perfume
127, 133, 145, 150, 151, 152, 153, 158, 166
Perfume (Formulators choice)
126
Perfume (Clean scent)
148
Perfume Cherry (Geranyl butyrate)
134
Perfume(scent)
126
Permethyl 101A
144
Permethyl 99A
144
pH
6, 8,- 11, 28, 29, 34, 37,38, 39, 41, 42, 68, 75, 78, 92, 98, 99, 103- 106, 114, 115, 126, 127
pH-Meter
10, 98, 99, 105
phosphate
17, 32, 41, 50, 51, 78, 89,114, 121
Phosphate ester
89
Phosphate Ester (monafax)
150

Phosphate Ester: Alcohol Ethoxylate
89
Phosphate Ester: Aliphatic
89
Phosphate Ester: Aromatic
89
Phosphate Ester: Linear Alcohol
89
Phosphate Ester: Linear Alcohol Alkoxylate
89
Phosphate Ester: Linear Alcohol Ethoxylate
89
Phosphate Ester: Nonylphenol Ethoxylate
89
Phosphate Ester: Polypropylene glycol Ethoxylate
89
Phosphoric acid
22, 31, 32, 50, 51, 105, 109, 128, 135, 137
Physical Mixing
118
PHYSICAL PROPERTIES
6, 60
Pickling
29, 31, 53, 76, 87
Pine oil
121, 123, 124
Plurafac D-25 Nonionic Surfactant
122
Plurafac RA-40 Nonionic Surfactant
122
Pluronic F 108
146, 147
Pluronic L-10
146
Pluronic L-61
127
Pluronic L-62
147
polarity
6, 18, 23, 113
Polidene 37-0065
136

Polyalkylene Glycol (Pluronic)
131
Polydimethylsiloxane (T SIL SF-20)
132
Polyethylene Glycol Dioleate
86
Polyethylene Glycol Oleate
86

polyprotic acids
103, 105
Polyrad 515
149
Polytergent SLF-18
158
Potassium
17, 36, 37, 46, 47, 48, 49, 50
Potassium carbonate
38, 41, 42
Potassium Chloride
46, 47
Potassium hydroxide
38, 41, 132, 141, 143, 152, 153, 166, 169
Potassium Oleate
154
Potassium pyrophosphate
121, 122, 123
Propylene Glycol
127, 146, 150
protic solvents
18, 192

Q

Qualitative analysis
10, 41, 105, 106
Quality control
21, 97, 105
Quaternary Ammonium, Chlorine
133

R

Randomization
93
Randomized test
94
Redox titration
105
Replication
93
Reversed phase
113

Rust removal
29, 32, 36, 37, 128, 135, 136

S

Sample size
94
Scent Lemon (Taylor 5006)
134
shear stress
6, 7, 91, 98
Silicone Emulsion SM 2059
166
Silicone Emulsion SM 2163*
166
Silicone emulsions
91
Silicone Fluid 18-350
164
Silicone Fluid SF
164
Silicone fluids
91
Sipex BOS Sulfate
125, 170
Siponic 218
170
Siponic L-12
170
Siponic SK
125, 141
Size exclusion chromatography
115
Sodium Alpha Olefin Sulfonate
80
Sodium Amphocarboxylate
75
Sodium Butoxy Ethyl Acetate
81
Sodium Capryloampho Propionate
76
Sodium carbonate
42, 43, 125, 126, 149, 158
Sodium Cetyl Sulfate
78
Sodium chloride
39, 44, 47, 100
Sodium Cocoampho Acetate
76
Sodium Cocoampho Hydroxypropyl Sulfonate
76
Sodium Cocoampho Propionate
76
Sodium Coconut N-Methyl Taurate
81
Sodium Cocoyl Isethionate
81

211

Sodium Dibutyl Naphthalene Sulfonate
80
Sodium Diisopropyl Naphthalene Sulfonate
80
Sodium Dinoyl Sulfosuccinate
80, 81
Sodium dodecyl benzene sulfonic acid
144
Sodium dodecyl sulfate
155, 156
Sodium Dodecylbenzene Sulfonate
80
Sodium hydroxide
38, 39, 40, 41, 76, 106, 126, 152, 157, 159
Sodium hypochlorite
132

Sodium Isodecyl Sulfate
78
Sodium Laureth Sulfate
79, 151, 152, 153, 166
Sodium Laureth Sulfonate
148, 151
Sodium Laurimino Dipropionate
77
Sodium Lauroampho Acetate
75
Sodium Lauryl Sulfate
78
Sodium Meta pyrophosphate
156

Sodium metasilicate
121, 122, 125, 141, 157, 169, 170
Sodium Metasilicate 5 Hydrate
152, 153, 164, 151
Sodium Methyl Cocoyl Taurate
81
Sodium nitrate
49, 50
Sodium Octyl Sulfate
78, 79
Sodium orthosilicate
155
Sodium o-silicate
169
Sodium persulfate
53
Sodium silicate
52
Sodium Sulfate
150, 158
Sodium Tall Oil Acid N Methyl Taurate
81

Sodium Tridecyl Sulfate
79
Sodium Tripolyphosphate
132, 133, 141,151, 152, 153, 157, 158, 166

Sodium Xylene Sulfonate (40%)
121, 122, 124, 125,148, 170
Sodium2-Ethylhexyl Sulfate
78
SOLUBILITY
6, 17,18, 40, 46, 60, 62, 68, 71, 84, 106, 167
Solubilization
68
Solutes
15, 18
Solvents
18, 21, 31, 35, 36, 40, 54, 55,56, 58, 61, 62, 86, 87, 88, 89, 111, 112, 113, 167
Sorbitan Monolaurate
86
Sorbitan Trioleate
86
Specialty surfactants
90
Specific gravity
6, 60, 63, 97
Spinning drop method
16
Stalagmometric method
16
Stepanate SODIUM XYLENE SULFONATE
169
Steric Stabilization
67
stokes
8
Stormer viscometer
7
Succinic acid
36
Sulfamic acid
33, 36, 37, 145, 148
Sulfate
17, 24, 50, 52, 53, 64
Sulfo-Ester
158
Sulfuric Acid (50%)
22, 23, 24, 25, 50, 52, 53, 57, 100, 138, 201
Surface tension
6, 13, 14, 15, 16, 61, 64, 68, 70, 91, 114
surfactant
15, 19, 21, 61, 64-91, 132, 133, 145
Surfamide 81
127, 152

212

Surfamide M-1
126, 152, 166
Surfonic N95
126, 127, 128, 130, 132, 133, 134, 137, 146, 148, 150, 157, 164, 165, 166, 168
Surfynol 104 H
136

T

Tall Oil Fatty Acid
127, 141
Tannic Acid
136
Tartaric acid
37
TDS conversion factor
102
Teflon Dispersion (Zonyl 7950)
139
Temperature compensation
102
Tergitol 15-S-5 Nonylphenol Ethoxylate
122, 128
Tergitol 24-L-60 Surfactant
125
Terpene
54, 56, 57, 130, 131
Tetra potassium pyrophosphate
147, 158
Thickener
71, 76, 85, 86
Tinopal CBS -X
158
Titration
28, 40, 41, 43, 103, 104, 105
Toluene
129

Tomah E-14-5
130
Toximul D-A
167
Toximul H-A
167

Trichlorethylene
129, 139, 140, 157
Triethanolamine
123, 126, 140, 150, 154, 159, 160
Triethanolamine
85   125

Triethanolamine Lauryl Sulfate
79
Trisodium Phosphate
124, 141, 154, 155, 157, 160, 161

Triton X-100
135, 136, 160, 161
Triton X-45
129, 130

U

UCON Fluid (5100)
142
Ultraviolet-visible spectroscopy
111, 112
Units of measure
116

V

Vaporization
107
velocity gradient
7, 118
Versene 100 Chelating agent
125, 143
Versene Acid
143
Viscasil 10M
164
Viscasil 60M
140
viscometer
7, 98
VISCOSITY
6, 7, 8, 21, 60, 68, 69, 71, 74, 76, 78, 84, 86, 91, 98, 118, 119
VM&P Naptha
159
Volatilization
107
Volume
6, 11, 13, 14, 16, 103, 104, 110, 112, 116, 119, 121

W

water
6- 10, 17- 19, 21- 62, 64, 66, 68 - 72, 73, 77, 79, 81, 83, 84, 86- 89, 91, 92, 97, 98, 101, 102, 106, 111- 113, 115, 118, 121-129, 131-170

213

Water softening
35
WAX emulsion
164
Wetting
15, 42, 66, 69, 71, 74,- 81, 84, 85, 86, 87, 88

Wilhelmy plate method 15
Witconate 1250 emulsifier
 122
Witconate 1260 emulsifier
122
Witconate K (Na DDBSA)
169

X
Xylene
124, 168

Z
Zahn cup
7

CPSIA information can be obtained
at www.ICGtesting.com
Printed in the USA
BVHW040821080719
R10088200001B/R100882PG552418BVX1B/1/P